FOLLOW ~ THE COAST —

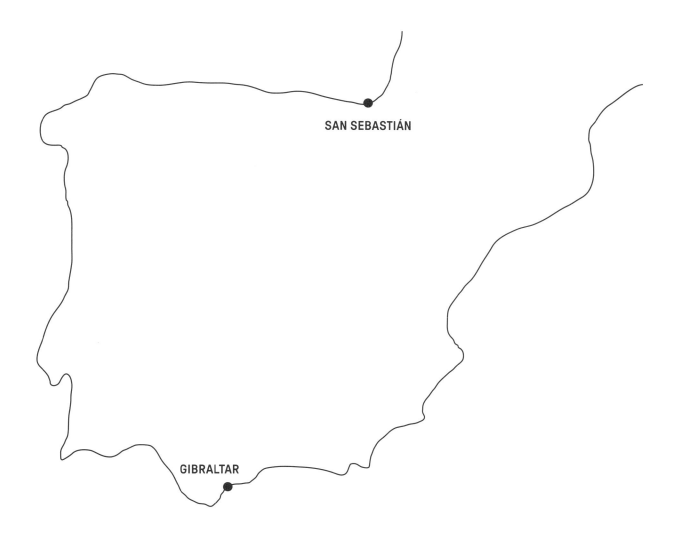

Camille Liebaert
Charles Van Haverbeke
Gert-Jan D'Haene
Lars Crommelinck
Max Monteyne

The Atlantic Coast
From San Sebastián to Gibraltar

TO MARK, KARIM & CÉLINE

Follow The Coast II
↳ Foreword

When Charles and I began this journey seven years ago, we had no idea what lay ahead. Today, seven years later, having ran and explored the coastline from Belgium to Gibraltar, countless stories have been shared and countless kilometres covered. I'm deeply honoured to be a vital part of this project and proud to address you here. We take immense pride in knowing that, as of this writing, we are the first project ever to document the running of 10,000 km of coastlines—anywhere, ever.

When Charles started writing the previous book, I noticed his fascination with lighthouses. He draws inspiration from these beacons of safety that have guided humanity for centuries, scattered along coastlines. Personally, over the course of this project, I've developed a healthy obsession of my own with another human creation: bridges. This foreword is a tribute to bridges. We can't imagine a coastline without them. Often, we take bridges for granted, but these technical marvels truly deserve our admiration. With every bridge we encounter—big or small, architectural wonder or not—I can't help but reflect on its beauty and the convenience it provides humanity. For me, a bridge is the ultimate symbol of connection

I like to believe that, like bridges, we connect with Follow the Coast. We connect people, stories, and stages. Within these books, we've connected 100 stages with the stories experienced by our runners, making Follow the Coast unique. So why does one run 100 km? I believe it's because it breaks you. Whether you're an experienced ultrarunner or a complete beginner, 100 km breaks you. Whether physically or mentally, it challenges you. The beauty of this "breaking," however, lies in the overcoming. Our runners conquer their own limits. They form a bridge over their boundaries and reach for the unknown shore on the other side. Helping them reach that shore is why we do what we do. That's the beauty we strive to capture and portray.

Follow the Coast began as a wild idea and has evolved into a story about friendship, emotion, and a quest for beauty. There are no glamorous finish lines, no crowds cheering along the way, no medals, no rewards, no official timings, and no podium. Our runners leave their egos behind at the start line. Follow the Coast doesn't run on ego; it runs on the sense of contributing to the bigger picture—being an essential part of an ever-growing chain. As a participant, you become the bridge between the stage before you and the stage ahead. I can tell you, being a bridge is an amazing and wondrous feeling.

I'm grateful to you, the reader, for contributing to our project by appreciating the beauty of this second book. I'm thankful for the over 150 runners who gave it their all to conquer 100 km of coastline and make it theirs for all eternity. I'm beyond grateful to our team—our talented photographers and designers, who have become true friends with whom I've shared countless adventures: thank you, Gert-Jan, Lars, Jules, Arthur, and Camille. You may be young, but your talents are undeniable.

To Charles: you're my inspiration, my friend, my partner in this project, and in the search for meaning, recognition, and beauty. I can't express how grateful I am to be part of your wild idea and to help bring it to life. Just like the many bridges in our ongoing story, we reached out from our own shore to connect and form this special bond, which serves as the foundation for this story. Being able to call you a true friend is a privilege.

Let's run the coast of Europe. Together.

Max

FOLLOW THE COAST
CAMILLE, CHARLES, JULES, GERT-JAN, LARS

BASQUE COUNTRY 12
CANTABRIA 36
ASTURIAS 72
GALICIA 190
NORTE 188
CENTRO 218
LISBON 250
ALENTEJO 284
ALGARVE 318
ANDALUSIA 352

Follow The Coast II
↳ Creators

Stage 47 - Harold-Jan Vanwijnsberghe, Arthur Vander Stichele
Stage 48 - Aaron Alonso
Stage 49 - Jelle Jacobs
Stage 50 - Koen Wilssens, Jeremy Genar
Stage 51 - *Not run yet. Scheduled later.*
Stage 52 - *Not run yet. Scheduled later.*
Stage 53 - Maarten Hermans, Sander Donders
Stage 54 - Federico Fiz, Stéphanie Cobbaert
Stage 55 - Sander De Deckere
Stage 56 - *Not run yet. Scheduled later.*
Stage 57 - Milan Cools
Stage 58 - Max Monteyne
Stage 59 - Jonathan Fors
Stage 60 - Tim Vroman, Aurillac Boury
Stage 61 - Stijn Boury, Gilles Lietaer
Stage 62 - *Not run yet. Scheduled later.*
Stage 63 - Max Monteyne
Stage 64 - Hung Nguyen
Stage 65 - Ann Vanden Wyngaerd, Ilse Vleminck
Stage 66 - *Not run yet. Scheduled later.*
Stage 67 - Anna Simonsson-Søndenå
Stage 68 - Federica Panzarella
Stage 69 - *Not run yet. Scheduled later.*
Stage 70 - Xander De Buysscher, Senne Vandevenne
Stage 71 - Federico Fiz

Stage 72 - *Not run yet. Scheduled later.*
Stage 73 - Igor Karpinski, Adrien Roose
Stage 74 - Lars Hanegraaf
Stage 75 - Charles Van Haverbeke
Stage 76 - Simon Corne
Stage 77 - Michiel Van Der Bauwhede
Stage 78 - Lode Van Laere, Wim Christiaens
Stage 79 - Gaetan D'Hondt
Stage 80 - Max Monteyne
Stage 81 - Cédric Spaas
Stage 82 - Céline Vervinckt, Ben Swerts, Pieterjan Van Leemputten, Olivier Wuyts
Stage 83 - Baptist Gilson, Arnaud Mertens
Stage 84 - Romy Kint, Nisrien Mortier
Stage 85 - Arthur Chambre, Amélie Harvengt
Stage 86 - Hugo Soares
Stage 87 - Richard Kruijskamp, Viktor Huegen
Stage 88 - Adam Wade
Stage 89 - Simon Corne
Stage 90 - Yeni Van den Bergh
Stage 91 - Joost Krijnen, Shiva Zanoli
Stage 92 - Charles Van Haverbeke
Stage 93 - Adrien Hardy
Stage 94 - Ramses De Weerdt
Stage 95 - Michiel Van Der Bauwhede

ART DIRECTION BY

Marcus Brown

CONTENT BY

Camille Liebaert, Charles Van Haverbeke, Max Monteyne

PHOTOGRAPHY BY

Gert-Jan D'Haene, Lars Crommelinck

WEBSITE BY

Pieter Delbeke

If you have any questions about the material in this book, please do not hesitate to contact our editorial team: art@lannoo.com
© Lannoo Publishers, Belgium, 2025
D/2025/45/29 – BISAC: TRV009000 / PHO023040
ISBN 9789020926446
All rights reserved. No part of this publication may be reproduced or transmitted in any form or by any means, electronic or mechanical, including photocopy, recording or any other information storage and retrieval system, without prior permission in writing from the publisher.

A visual travel guide

↳ This book is your perfect guide to discover the beauty of the Atlantic coast of Spain & Portugal. You will find incredible images and practical tips & tricks on hidden gems along the way. The book is divided in 10 regions, which are subdivided again in "stages", with 100 km of coastline each. Every region section contains information on the culture, how to get around and key highlights you can't miss. Each Stage section features a clear map, local highlights, and guidelines, while also sharing the inspiring stories of those who run the 100km.

The second chapter

↳ We created this book by doing a relay run along the coast of Europe. We divided the coast into stretches of 100 km which can be claimed by a team of runners who have 24h to run their Stage. The runners are followed by a team of professional photographers who capture the beauty we encounter during our collective journey. We started our collective journey on 1th July 2019. We survived Covid and we reached Gibraltar in March 2024.

In 2021, we published our first book, covering the French Atlantic coast from Belgium to San Sebastián, of which we sold out the first edition. We are proud to publish our second book in Spring 2025 on the Iberian Atlantic coast, from San Sebastián to Gibraltar. In 2025, we will run all the Mediterranean coast of Spain and France and publish a third book, likely at the end of 2025 or 2026. The fourth book will cover the entire Italian coast. We plan to continue like this, covering 3,000 or more kilometres per year until we cover the entire coastline of Europe.

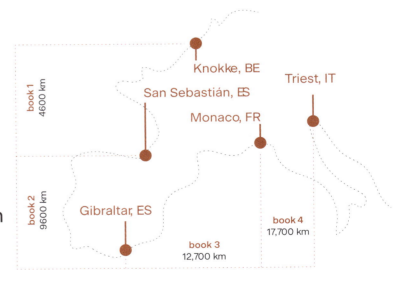

Follow The Coast II
↳ Overview

To help you find your favourite spot, we have created a handy overview and map. Below is an overview map with the locations of the start of every stage and the 'best of' highlights we selected. On the right page, you can see the list of Stages with the start & finish locations, joined with our evaluation on a handful of criteria.

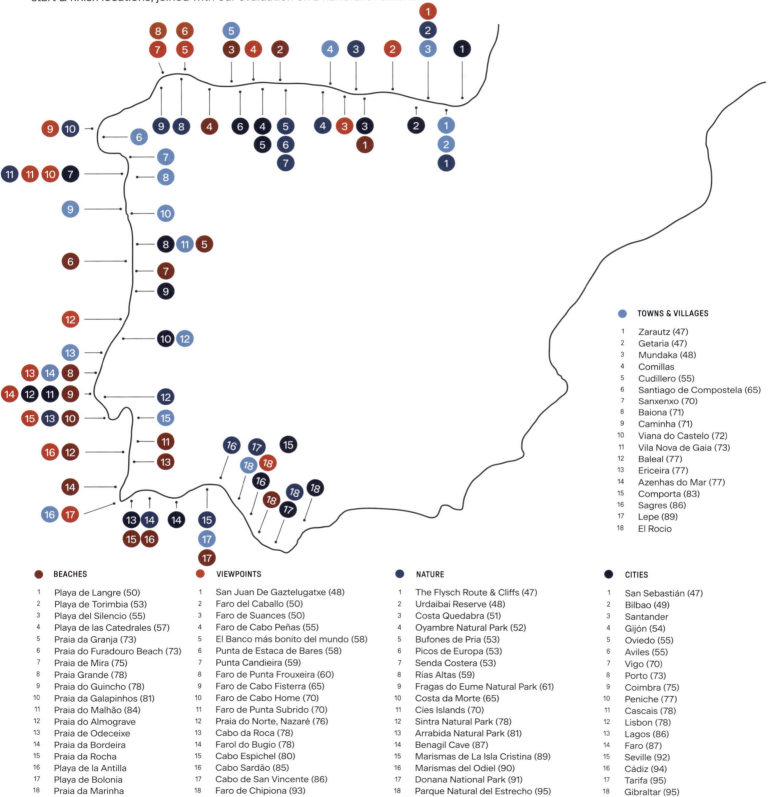

TOWNS & VILLAGES

1. Zarautz (47)
2. Getaria (47)
3. Mundaka (48)
4. Comillas
5. Cudillero (55)
6. Santiago de Compostela (65)
7. Sanxenxo (70)
8. Baiona (71)
9. Caminha (71)
10. Viana do Castelo (72)
11. Vila Nova de Gaia (73)
12. Baleal (77)
13. Ericeira (77)
14. Azenhas do Mar (77)
15. Comporta (83)
16. Sagres (86)
17. Lepe (89)
18. El Rocio

BEACHES

1. Playa de Langre (50)
2. Playa de Torimbia (53)
3. Playa del Silencio (55)
4. Playa de las Catedrales (57)
5. Praia da Granja (73)
6. Praia do Furadouro Beach (73)
7. Praia de Mira (75)
8. Praia Grande (78)
9. Praia do Guincho (78)
10. Praia da Galapinhos (81)
11. Praia do Malhão (84)
12. Praia do Almograve
13. Praia de Odeceixe
14. Praia da Bordeira
15. Praia da Rocha
16. Playa de la Antilla
17. Playa de Bolonia
18. Praia da Marinha

VIEWPOINTS

1. San Juan De Gaztelugatxe (48)
2. Faro del Caballo (50)
3. Faro de Suances (50)
4. Faro de Cabo Peñas (55)
5. El Banco más bonito del mundo (58)
6. Punta de Estaca de Bares (58)
7. Punta Candieira (59)
8. Faro de Punta Frouxeira (60)
9. Faro de Cabo Fisterra (65)
10. Faro de Cabo Home (70)
11. Faro de Punta Subrido (70)
12. Praia do Norte, Nazaré (76)
13. Cabo da Roca (78)
14. Farol do Bugio (78)
15. Cabo Espichel (80)
16. Cabo Sardão (85)
17. Cabo de San Vincente (86)
18. Faro de Chipiona (93)

NATURE

1. The Flysch Route & Cliffs (47)
2. Urdaibai Reserve (48)
3. Costa Quedabra (51)
4. Oyambre Natural Park (52)
5. Bufones de Pria (53)
6. Picos de Europa (53)
7. Senda Costera (53)
8. Rías Altas (59)
9. Fragas do Eume Natural Park (61)
10. Costa da Morte (65)
11. Cies Islands (70)
12. Sintra Natural Park (78)
13. Arrabida Natural Park (81)
14. Benagil Cave (87)
15. Marismas de La Isla Cristina (89)
16. Marismas del Odiel (90)
17. Donana National Park (91)
18. Parque Natural del Estrecho (95)

CITIES

1. San Sebastián (47)
2. Bilbao (49)
3. Santander
4. Gijón (54)
5. Oviedo (55)
6. Aviles (55)
7. Vigo (70)
8. Porto (73)
9. Coimbra (75)
10. Peniche (77)
11. Cascais (78)
12. Lisbon (78)
13. Lagos (86)
14. Faro (87)
15. Seville (92)
16. Cádiz (94)
17. Tarifa (95)
18. Gibraltar (95)

Legend: ● = Best-in-class, ◐ = Great, ○ = Not recommended

Region	Stage	From	To	Page	Wonders of nature	City trip	Lovely village	History	Architecture	Beach	Overall
BASQUE COUNTRY	47	San Sebastián	Playa Laida	28	●	●	●	●	●	●	●
	48	Playa Laida	Barakaldo	32	◐	○	○	●	◐	◐	◐
CANTABRIA	49	Barakaldo	Colindres	56	●	●	◐	●	●	○	●
	50	Colindres	Santander	60	●	◐	○	●	◐	◐	●
	51	Santander	Playa de la Tablía	64	●	◐	○	●	○	●	●
	52	Playa de la Tablía	Puertas de Vidiago	68	◐	○	◐	●	◐	◐	●
ASTURIAS	53	Puertas de Vidiago	Santa Mera	90	●	○	○	◐	○	●	●
	54	Santa Mera	Bañugues	94	◐	○	◐	◐	◐	◐	◐
	55	Bañugues	Castañeras	98	●	◐	●	●	●	◐	●
	56	Castañeras	San Antonio	102	●	○	◐	●	◐	●	●
GALICIA	57	San Antonio	Lago	130	●	○	○	◐	○	●	◐
	58	Lago	O Mosteiro	134	●	○	○	○	○	◐	◐
	59	O Mosteiro	Cala Burbujas, O Barral	138	●	○	○	○	○	●	◐
	60	Cala Burbujas, O Barral	Ferrol	142	●	○	◐	●	◐	◐	◐
	61	Ferrol	Punta Torrella	146	◐	◐	◐	◐	●	◐	◐
	62	Punta Torrella	Punta Falsa, Buno	150	●	○	◐	○	○	●	◐
	63	Punta Falsa, Buno	Arou	154	●	○	○	○	○	●	◐
	64	Arou	Frixe	158	●	○	◐	○	○	●	◐
	65	Frixe	Punta Cantón	162	●	○	◐	◐	○	◐	◐
	66	Punta Cantón	Corrubedo	166	●	○	◐	○	○	●	●
	67	Corrubedo	Catoira	170	◐	○	◐	●	◐	○	◐
	68	Catoira	Illa da Toxa	174	●	○	◐	◐	◐	◐	◐
	69	Illa da Toxa	Cabo Udra	178	●	◐	◐	○	●	◐	◐
	70	Cabo Udra	Patos	182	●	○	◐	○	◐	◐	◐
	71	Patos	Fontela	186	◐	○	○	○	◐	◐	◐
NORTE	72	Fontela	Mindelo	206	◐	○	●	●	●	◐	●
	73	Mindelo	São Jacinto	210	●	○	◐	●	●	●	●
	74	São Jacinto	Praia da Costa Nova	214	◐	○	●	◐	◐	●	●
CENTRO	75	Praia da Costa Nova	Pedrógão	238	◐	●	○	◐	○	●	●
	76	Pedrógão	Lagos de Óbidos	242	●	○	○	○	○	●	◐
	77	Lagos de Óbidos	Azenhas do Mar	246	●	○	◐	●	◐	●	●
LISBON	78	Azenhas do Mar	Samora Correia, Lisbon	272	●	●	◐	●	●	●	●
	79	Samora Correia, Lisbon	Verderena, Lisbon	276	○	◐	○	●	◐	○	◐
	80	Verderena, Lisbon	Praia do Inferno, Sesimbra	280	●	◐	◐	◐	◐	●	◐
ALENTEJO	81	Praia do Inferno, Sesimbra	Gâmbia, Setubal	302	●	◐	◐	◐	◐	●	●
	82	Gâmbia, Setubal	Moitinha, Comporta	306	◐	○	○	○	○	●	◐
	83	Moitinha, Comporta	Praia da Aberta Nova, Melides	310	◐	○	○	○	○	●	◐
	84	Praia da Aberta Nova, Melides	Almograve	314	◐	○	○	○	○	●	◐
ALGARVE	85	Almograve	Praia do Amado	336	●	○	◐	○	○	●	●
	86	Praia do Amado	Praia da Rocha	340	●	○	◐	○	○	●	●
	87	Praia da Rocha	Olhão	344	◐	◐	◐	○	◐	●	●
	88	Olhão	Isla Canela, Ayamonte	348	◐	○	●	◐	◐	◐	◐
ANDALUSIA	89	Isla Canela, Ayamonte	Lepe	370	●	○	◐	◐	○	●	◐
	90	Lepe	Mazagón	374	◐	○	◐	◐	○	◐	◐
	91	Mazagón	Isla Minima	378	◐	○	◐	●	◐	○	◐
	92	Isla Minima	Lebrija	382	◐	○	●	◐	◐	○	◐
	93	Lebrija	Puerto Real	386	○	◐	●	●	◐	○	◐
	94	Puerto Real	Camarinal	390	◐	●	◐	●	●	◐	●
	95	Camarinal	Gibraltar	394	◐	●	●	●	◐	●	●

● BEST-IN-CLASS ◐ GREAT ○ NOT RECOMMENDED

↪ Regions 1 / 10
Basque Country

7,234 km²
2,227,000 inhabitants

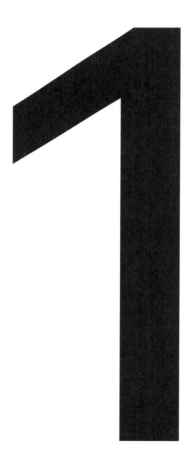

→ FLYSCH ROCKS

↳ The Basque Country is a relatively small but true gem, featuring small beaches and numerous rugged coves nestled among lush green hills that rise into the Pyrenees mountains. These peaks are so close to the coast that swift rivers weave through the region, carving out dramatic cliffs and rugged coastlines.

With its picturesque bay and promenade, San Sebastián is a romantic hotspot and a favourite destination for those who enjoy surfing and tapas. Bilbao, the Basque Country's largest city, is a river port boasting international acclaim, largely thanks to the famous Guggenheim Museum. The area is also a foodie hotspot, with world-renowned restaurants and local specialities including Txakoli wine, cider, and pintxos, the popular bite-size snacks named after the toothpicks that characterise them.

The region has a mild climate, with average temperatures of 25°C in the summer, but it is also known for its abundant rainfall – a blessing in sun-parched Spain – which results in truly lush landscapes.

Basque Country	256km Coastline
	Capital: Vitoria-Gasteiz

Basque Country
↳ Introduction

HOW TO GET THERE

The Basque Country is well-connected internationally through its three airports. Bilbao Airport (BIO), the main gateway to the region, is located about 12 km north of Bilbao and offers numerous international and domestic flights. San Sebastián Airport (EAS), situated near the French border, primarily provides flights to and from other Spanish destinations. Vitoria Airport (VIT), near Vitoria-Gasteiz, serves fewer flights but can be a convenient option for travellers.

Additionally, both Bilbao and San Sebastián have train stations that connect them to cities in Spain and beyond.

WHERE TO STAY

The Basque coastline is dotted with a variety of charming cities and towns that provide visitors with a range of experiences and places to stay.

Located on the French-Spanish border, the historic town of Hondarribia is known for its well-preserved old quarter. The cobblestone streets and ancient walls give it unique character, making it a delightful place to explore.

Known as Donostia in Basque, San Sebastián is famous for its stunning beaches like La Concha and Zurriola, which attract visitors from around the world. It's a vibrant blend of urban sophistication and coastal charm, renowned for its world-class culinary scene, including numerous Michelin-starred restaurants. Whether you're strolling along the beach promenade or enjoying pintxos in the lively old town, San Sebastián offers a perfect mix of relaxation and excitement.

Although primarily an urban centre, Bilbao is conveniently located near coastal areas and provides a different kind of experience. The city is a hub of culture, with attractions such as the iconic Guggenheim Museum drawing art lovers from everywhere. Its dynamic nightlife and diverse dining options make it a great base for those who want to combine cultural exploration with coastal visits.

For those seeking a quieter, more relaxed atmosphere, Getaria is a picturesque fishing village known for its fresh seafood and beautiful coastal views. It offers a tranquil retreat with its charming harbour, narrow streets, and rich maritime heritage. It's the perfect spot to unwind and savour the simple pleasures of the Basque coast.

Finally, Mundaka is a small town that has gained international fame for its world-renowned surf spot where the river meets the ocean. This charming town attracts surfers and nature lovers alike, offering a peaceful setting with breathtaking views. Whether you're there to catch waves or simply enjoy the natural beauty, Mundaka embodies the laid-back, adventurous spirit of the Basque coast.

HISTORY

The Basque Country, or Euskal Herria in the native language, is a region steeped in history and culture. The Basque people are one of the oldest ethnic groups in Europe, while their language, Euskara, is unique and unrelated to any other language in the world, predating even the Roman Empire. This deep-rooted cultural heritage is woven into the fabric of the region, from its architecture and traditions to its festivals and way of life.

Throughout history, the Basque people have maintained a strong sense of identity and autonomy, which is evident in the region's distinctive culture and customs. The Basque Country's rich history is not only reflected in its language and traditions but also in its landscapes, cities, and towns. From the historic streets of Hondarribia to the modern art of Bilbao, the Basque Country offers a fascinating journey through time, where the past and present coexist in perfect harmony.

BASQUE COUNTRY

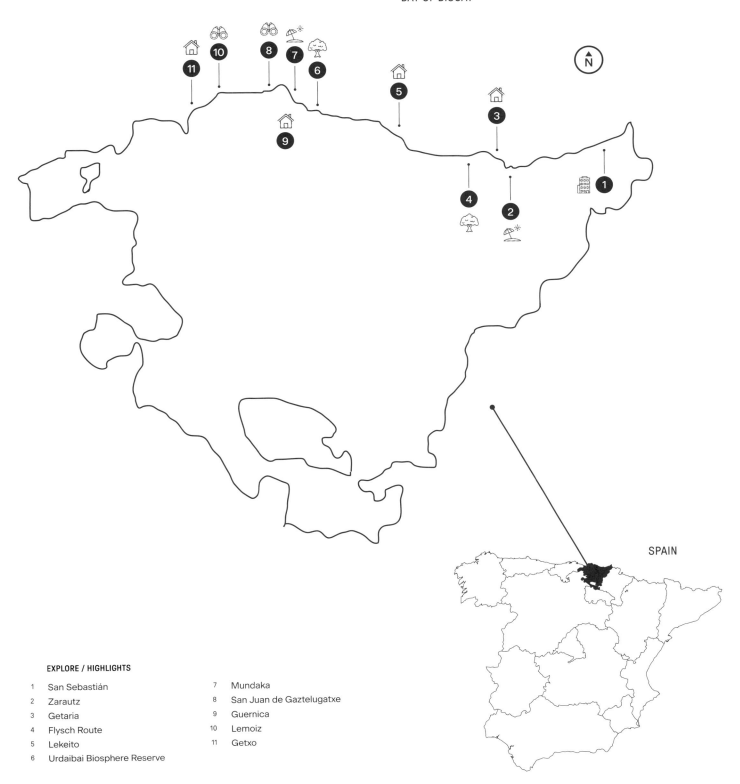

EXPLORE / HIGHLIGHTS

1. San Sebastián
2. Zarautz
3. Getaria
4. Flysch Route
5. Lekeito
6. Urdaibai Biosphere Reserve
7. Mundaka
8. San Juan de Gaztelugatxe
9. Guernica
10. Lemoiz
11. Getxo

Basque Country
↳ Highlights

Nestled between the rugged peaks of the Pyrenees and the azure waters of the Bay of Biscay, the Basque Country is a region where nature's grandeur and diversity are on full display. This unique area offers a rich tapestry of landscapes, from dramatic cliffs and sweeping beaches to lush forests and serene wetlands.

The region's coastline is particularly captivating, with its blend of natural beauty, historical significance and cultural charm. As you journey along the Basque coast, you'll encounter a variety of breathtaking environments – each telling its own story through its scenery, geology and the vibrant communities that call it home.

Whether you're a lover of the outdoors, a history enthusiast, or simply someone seeking tranquillity by the sea, the Basque Country's natural splendour provides an unforgettable experience.

1. SAN SEBASTIÁN

San Sebastián, or Donostia, is the jewel of the Basque coastline, renowned for its blend of urban sophistication and natural beauty. La Concha Beach, one of Europe's most famous urban beaches, is a stunning crescent-shaped bay with golden sand and calm waters, perfect for swimming and relaxation. Overlooking the city, Mount Igeldo offers panoramic views of San Sebastián and the bay. Accessible by a funicular railway, the top of Mount Igeldo is a must-visit for breathtaking scenery, with the city's elegant architecture framed by the endless expanse of the Atlantic Ocean.

2. ZARAUTZ

With its long, sandy beach, Zarautz is one of the Basque Country's premier surfing destinations. The consistent waves and beautiful setting make it a favourite spot for surfers of all levels. Beyond the beach, Zarautz is a lively town with plenty of restaurants, bars and cultural attractions, making it a great place to experience the local way of life.

3. GETARIA

Just a short drive away, the charming fishing village of Getaria offers a more relaxed seaside experience. Its Gaztetape Beach is perfect for a peaceful day by the sea. The village is also home to the historic Church of San Salvador, and a museum dedicated to fashion designer and Getaria native Cristóbal Balenciaga. With its cobblestone streets, fresh seafood and picturesque views, Getaria is a delightful escape for those looking to enjoy the slower pace of coastal life.

4. FLYSCH ROUTE

Spanning from Zumaia to Mutriku through Deba, the Flysch Route, or Ruta del Flysch, is a geological wonder that showcases the Earth's history through its impressive cliffs and unique rock formations. Known as Flysch, these layers of sedimentary rock were formed over millions of years and offer a fascinating glimpse into the planet's past. The best way to experience this natural marvel is by taking a coastal hike or a boat tour along the Flysch Route.

Itzurun Beach in Zumaia, with its towering cliffs and otherworldly formations, is a highlight of this route and has even been featured in the TV series *Game of Thrones*. Whether you're a geology enthusiast or simply someone who appreciates breathtaking landscapes, the Flysch Route is an unforgettable experience.

5. LEKEITIO

Lekeitio is a tranquil town on the Basque coast, known for its beautiful Isuntza Beach and the nearby San Nicolás Island. At low tide, visitors can walk across a causeway to the small island, which offers panoramic views of the town and the surrounding coastline. Lekeitio's peaceful atmosphere, combined with its natural beauty, makes it an ideal destination for those looking to relax and soak in the serene coastal environment.

6. URDAIBAI BIOSPHERE RESERVE

The Urdaibai Biosphere Reserve, a UNESCO-listed site near Gernika, is a paradise for nature lovers. This diverse area encompasses wetlands, forests, beaches, and coastal cliffs, creating a rich tapestry of ecosystems. Birdwatchers will find the reserve particularly rewarding, as it is home to numerous species of birds, including migratory ones.

The Urdaibai Reserve offers a variety of trails and viewpoints, allowing visitors to explore its natural beauty at their own pace. From the serene estuaries to the lush woodlands, Urdaibai is a place where the tranquillity of nature can be fully embraced, making it a must-visit for those seeking a deeper connection with nature.

7. MUNDAKA

Famous worldwide for its legendary surf spot where the river meets the ocean, Mundaka is a pilgrimage site for surfers, drawn by the perfect waves and the vibrant surfing community. Despite its fame in the surfing world, Mundaka retains a laid-back, small-town charm, with narrow streets, traditional Basque houses, and sea views. Whether you're there to catch the perfect wave or simply to enjoy the coastal scenery, Mundaka is a must-visit for surf enthusiasts and nature lovers alike.

8. SAN JUAN DE GAZTELUGATXE

Perched atop a rocky islet off the coast near Bermeo, San Juan de Gaztelugatxe is one of the most iconic and picturesque spots in the Basque Country. This hermitage, dedicated to Saint John the Baptist and probably dating back to the 9th century, is accessible via a dramatic, narrow bridge and staircase that winds its way up from the beach. The climb, while challenging, rewards visitors with breathtaking views and a sense of achievement. With stunning views of the coastline and the vast Atlantic Ocean, the site is particularly enchanting at sunset, when the sky is painted with hues of orange and pink.

9. GERNIKA

The Basque coastline is not only rich in natural beauty but also steeped in history and culture. Gernika, a small town made famous by Picasso's haunting painting depicting its bombing during the Spanish Civil War, is a poignant reminder of the region's turbulent past. Visitors can explore the Peace Museum and the famous Gernika Tree, a symbol of Basque freedom and identity.

10. LEMOIZ

For those interested in more offbeat sites, the abandoned nuclear power plant in Lemoiz offers a fascinating glimpse into the region's industrial past. The site, with its eerie, unfinished structures and stunning views of the coastline, is a hidden gem for those who appreciate abandoned places and the stories they hold.

11. GETXO

In Getxo, visitors can explore the old harbour town at the mouth of the Nervión River, which connects it to Bilbao. The town is home to the iconic Vizcaya Bridge, a UNESCO World Heritage site and the world's oldest transporter bridge. A marvel of engineering, this iron structure supports a suspended gondola that ferries cars and passengers between Getxo and Portugalete, and offers stunning views of the river and the surrounding area. Getxo's blend of historical significance and coastal charm makes it a fascinating destination for those exploring the Basque Country.

URDAIBAI SANCTUARY

⌞ ISLA DE SAN NICOLAS LEKEITIOKO ⌝

Stage 47

SAN SEBASTIÁN > PLAYA LAIDA

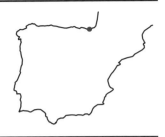

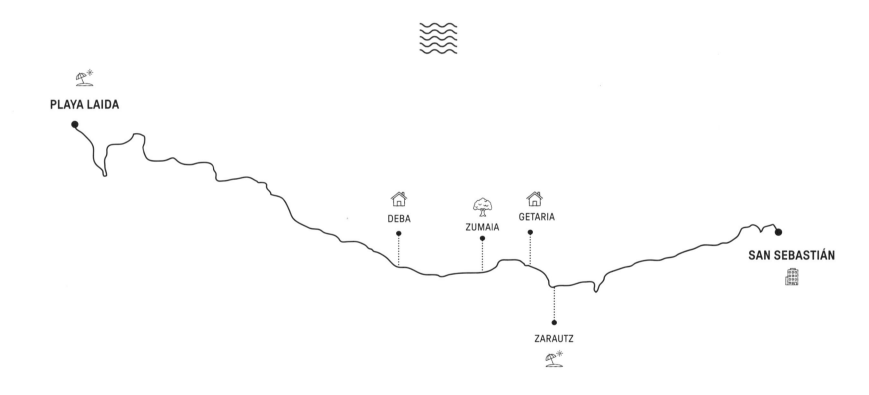

DATE	30/04/2022
DISTANCE	100.58 KM
ELEVATION	2,105 M
TOTAL TIME	16H32
MOVING TIME	14H48

SHOREHOLDERS
Harold-Jan Vanwijnsberghe
Arthur Vander Stichele

ISUNTZA HONDARTZA, LEKEITIOKO

STAGE HIGHLIGHTS

 San Sebastián - Donostia
Vibrant city, known for its culinary scene, from the famous pintxos to the Michelin star restaurant.. Visit La Concha Beach, known for its crescent shape and picturesque bay views.

 Getaria
Charming town on a rocky peninsula, celebrated for its fishing heritage and delicious seafood. A stroll through its quaint streets leads you to Getaria Beach, framed by lush cliffs.

 Zarautz
Surfers town, famous for its long sandy beach, for surfers and sunbathers.

 Sanctuary of Itziar - Deba
Provides panoramic views of the coastline.

 Mutriku
Charming port town known for its seafood.

 Flysch cliffs of Zumaia
Remarkable geological formations and stunning vistas along the Itzurun Beach and Flysch route, renowned for its appearance in *Game of Thrones*.

STAGE STORY

"The sun rises over the Bay of Biscay, painting the horizon in strokes of gold and orange. The coastal air is crisp and invigorating, and the rhythmic sound of crashing waves echoes in the distance. Harold-Jan and Arthur exchange a quick smile as they stand at the trailhead in San Sebastián. The adventure begins.

The first stretch feels almost too easy. Their strides are confident, fuelled by adrenaline and excitement. They tackle the early kilometres with enthusiasm, the rocky cliffs and emerald waters offering breathtaking views. Each step is a reminder of why they chose this challenge—a test of endurance against a backdrop of nature's finest.

As they push deeper into the course, the terrain becomes unforgiving. Narrow, winding paths hug steep cliffs. Unreachable roads force them to slow down. At one point, they lose their way, the trail markers seemingly vanishing in the dense undergrowth. Frustration bubbles. Time ticks by.

By midday, the sun is merciless. Sweat streaks their faces, their breathing laboured. Harold-Jan's parents appear at a checkpoint, offering cold water and encouragement. Their support is a lifeline. Max, their ever-enthusiastic friend, cheers from the sidelines, his energy a welcome counterbalance to the creeping exhaustion.

Arthur's legs cramp. His body threatens rebellion, the pain sharp and persistent. Salted chips, painkillers, and a gulp of Red Bull become a quick remedy. Harold-Jan's mother helps him during a brief stop, while his father runs alongside for a few kilometres, setting a steady pace.

For Harold-Jan, the low comes later. The miles stretch endlessly, his mind questioning every step. Is it worth it? Should they stop? Arthur, revived from his earlier setback, offers words of encouragement. Together, they press on, pain now a constant companion.

Finally, the horizon shifts. The finish line beckons from Gametxo Auzoa. The sight stirs a second wind, and the pair dig deep into reserves they didn't know they had. The last kilometres blur—agonising yet exhilarating.

And then, it's over.

They stumble across the finish line, side by side. A wave of relief washes over them as cold beers are thrust into their hands. Exhausted but victorious, they savour the moment, knowing they've shared an experience that will stay with them forever."

Stage 48

PLAYA LAIDA > BARAKALDO

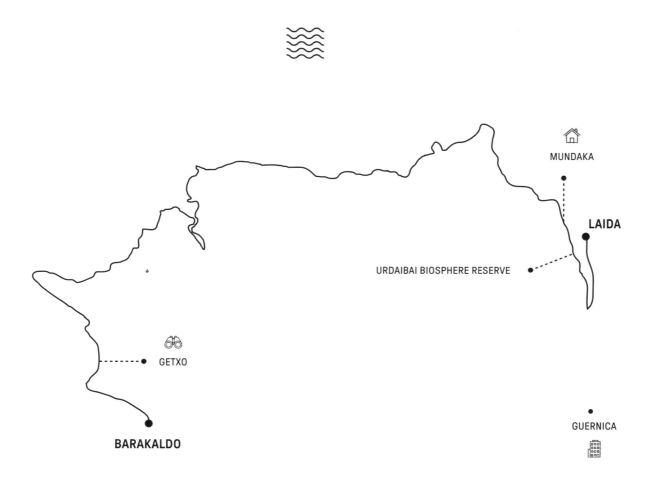

DATE	01/05/2022
DISTANCE	88.03 KM
ELEVATION	2,499 M
TOTAL TIME	11H02
MOVING TIME	9H03

SHOREHOLDER
Aaron Alonso

SAN JUAN DE GAZTELUGATXE

STAGE HIGHLIGHTS

 Guernica
Holds deep historical significance, famously immortalised by Picasso's painting after the tragic bombing in the Spanish Civil War.

 Mundaka
Charming beach side village with world-class waves.

 San Juan de Gaztelugatxe
Hermitage perched atop a rocky islet. Famous for its role as Dragonstone in *Game of Thrones*, its zigzagging staircase and ocean views make it a must-see.

 Lemoizko Zentral Nuklearra
An abandoned nuclear plant, offers haunting coastal views for those interested in forgotten industrial history.

 Geltokiko Zubia
Suspension bridge in Plentzia provides sweeping river views.

 Vizcaya Bridge, Getxo
A UNESCO-listed transporter bridge, marks the end of this unforgettable adventure.

STAGE STORY

Truth be told, my participation in Follow the Coast was spontaneous. I stumbled upon the project on social media and, seeing a stage running through my Basque Country home turf, I knew I had to join. It was the perfect chance to link my favourite local routes into one epic adventure—a challenge I'd envisioned for years.

The day began with a golden sunrise over Urdaibai. Clear skies, cool air—ideal running conditions. The first stretch was unfamiliar territory, with narrow trails and occasional road crossings demanding focus. Determined to start strong, I pushed the pace and arrived in Bermeo earlier than expected, where my first running companion, Urtzi Martinez, joined me. Together, we ran the cliff-hugging paths toward San Juan de Gaztelugatxe, the sea crashing below us.

In Bakio, our group grew. Jon Galbarriartu and Lisa Worthington joined us just in time for the toughest leg—rolling hills and steep climbs toward Armintza. Lisa had her doubts about joining, but her energy and laughter brought fresh momentum to our team. A pit stop in Armintza provided much-needed fuel, and a food truck serving oysters delighted the supporters waiting for us.

With new companions, Oier Urrutia, Aitor Egiluz, and Lander Unanue, I set off for Sopela, my hometown. These were familiar trails, part of my regular training runs. We picked up the pace, legs aching but hearts light, knowing the finish line wasn't far.

From Sopela to the Hanging Bridge of Getxo, I ran solo. Instead of feeling alone, I found peace, reflecting on the journey—the camaraderie, the beauty of the Basque coast, and the support of friends and family. As the iconic bridge came into view, cheers erupted, and a cold Duvel awaited me at the finish line.

Lisa, who tackled her 8 km section with determination, later said it was an incredible way to experience the coastline. "Before moving here, I'd barely run a hill in my life. But Aaron inspired me—and who knows? Maybe I'll run a full stage someday."

For me, this wasn't just about running. It was about the people, the landscape, and the shared passion for this incredible mission. To Max, Gert-Jan, and the entire Follow the Coast team: may the journey continue for many more kilometres ahead.

↱ Regions 2 / 10
Cantabria

5,321 km²
581,000 inhabitants

→ PICOS DE EUROPA

CABO DE GALIZANO - LANGRE

↳ Cantabria's stunning coastline blends natural beauty with rich history. To the west, the Cantabrian Mountains stretch over 300 kilometres, their rugged peaks framing the region. Near Santander, cliffs and hills offer breathtaking views, with the trail between Oriñón and Laredo perfect for invigorating walks.

Santander, a lively port city, is known for landmarks like the Palacio de la Magdalena. Westward, the landscape softens, revealing tranquil beaches near the Asturias border, ideal for a peaceful retreat. Comillas stands out with unique architecture, including Gaudí's El Capricho villa and the Pontifical University, overlooking the coast.

Cantabria's abundant rainfall nurtures lush vegetation, creating a rich diversity of plant life. This, combined with dramatic topography, makes the coastline a paradise for outdoor enthusiasts, with dunes, rocky outcrops, secluded beaches, and peaceful estuaries to explore.

Cantabria

220km Coastline
Capital: Santander

Cantabria
↳ Introduction

HOW TO GET THERE

Cantabria is well-connected and easily accessible, with its main transportation hubs located in the capital city of Santander. Santander Airport (SDR), situated just about 5 km from the city centre, offers flights to various national and international destinations, making it a convenient option for travellers from across Europe and beyond.

For those preferring to travel by train, Santander Railway Station provides direct national connections, though it does not offer international routes.

WHERE TO STAY

Cantabria's coastline is dotted with charming towns and cities, each offering unique experiences and accommodations to suit every traveller's taste.

As the capital of Cantabria, Santander is a vibrant city that perfectly blends urban sophistication with natural beauty. It boasts excellent beaches, such as Playa del Sardinero, and expansive parks like the Jardines de Piquío. Cultural attractions include the iconic Palacio de la Magdalena, situated on a peninsula of the same name, and the modern art centre, Centro Botín, a must-visit for art lovers. With its dynamic atmosphere and picturesque surroundings, Santander is a perfect base for exploring the region.

Castro Urdiales is a beautiful harbour town steeped in history, with medieval roots that are still visible today. Its skyline is dominated by the imposing Santa María de la Asunción Church and the Castle of Santa Ana, which also features a lighthouse. Castro Urdiales offers a blend of historical charm and coastal beauty, making it a delightful place to stay for those interested in Cantabria's rich past.

Known as a university village, Comillas is a unique blend of coastal charm and cultural heritage. Once a retreat for Spanish royalty and nobility, Comillas is home to an array of impressive buildings, including Gaudí's whimsical El Capricho villa, the stately Palacio de Sobrellano, the historic University of Comillas, and the Casa del Duque de Almodóvar del Río. The town's architectural splendour, combined with its serene coastal setting, makes it a standout destination in Cantabria.

Laredo is famous for its long, sandy beach, Playa de la Salvé, which stretches for several kilometres. The town also offers a variety of water sports and outdoor activities, making it an ideal destination for those looking to enjoy Cantabria's natural beauty.

The charming fishing town of San Vicente de la Barquera offers stunning views of the Picos de Europa mountains and a scenic estuary. Its serene environment and natural beauty make it an excellent choice for those seeking a peaceful retreat.

HISTORY

Cantabria is a region with a rich and varied history, dating back to prehistoric times. The name "Cantabria" itself is derived from the ancient Celtic tribe of the Cantabri, who fiercely resisted Roman conquest in the first century BC. Throughout the Middle Ages, Cantabria was a strategic location, as evidenced by the many castles and fortifications that dot its landscape. Its coastal towns, such as Castro Urdiales and Santander, played crucial roles in maritime trade and defence.

Today, Cantabria preserves its rich cultural heritage while also embracing modernity, offering visitors a unique glimpse into the past alongside contemporary attractions. The region's history is reflected in its stunning architecture, ancient traditions, and the deep connection its people have with the land and sea.

CANTABRIA

EXPLORE / HIGHLIGHTS

1. Faro del Caballo
2. Monte Buciero
3. Playa de Langre
4. Costa Quebrada Geological Park
5. Suances Peninsula
6. Oyambre Natural Park
7. El Soplao Cave
8. Tina Menor Estuary

REGION 2 / 10

PLAYA DE VALDEARENAS

Cantabria
↳ Highlights

The coastline of Cantabria, tucked away in northern Spain, is a treasure trove of natural wonders, where rugged cliffs meet tranquil beaches and dramatic rock formations create stunning seascapes.

1. FARO DEL CABALLO

Perched on a sheer cliff, the isolated Faro del Caballo, or Horse Lighthouse, is one of Cantabria's most striking landmarks. It is accessible via a steep, winding staircase with 764 steps, ascending from sea level to over 200 m high, a journey both physically demanding and visually rewarding, as it offers breathtaking views of the rugged coastline and the endless ocean.

The lighthouse itself, situated in an almost untouched setting, provides a dramatic and memorable experience. The effort to reach it is well worth the spectacular panoramas and the sense of achievement upon arrival.

2. MONTE BUCIERO

Located near Santoña, Monte Buciero is a prominent headland offering breathtaking views of the Cantabrian coast. The mountain is covered in dense forests of oak and beech, with trails that lead to hidden coves and secluded beaches.

One of the highlights of Monte Buciero is the Fort of San Martín, an ancient fortress that offers panoramic views of the Bay of Santoña and the surrounding coastline. The combination of historical interest and natural beauty makes Monte Buciero a compelling destination for hikers and history enthusiasts alike.

3. PLAYA DE LANGRE

Often considered one of Cantabria's hidden gems, Playa de Langre is a secluded beach surrounded by towering cliffs. The beach is renowned for its pristine sands and crystal-clear waters, making it a popular spot for surfers and beachgoers alike. The dramatic cliffs that enclose the beach add to its allure, creating a natural amphitheatre that enhances the sense of isolation and tranquillity. The beach is a perfect destination for those looking to escape the crowds and immerse themselves in the natural beauty of Cantabria's coastline.

4. COSTA QUEBRADA GEOLOGICAL PARK

Just west of Santander lies the Costa Quebrada, a natural park that showcases the raw beauty of Cantabria's coastline. This area is renowned for its distinctive Flysch rock formations, which are a testament to millions of years of geological activity. The coastline here is characterised by rugged cliffs, sweeping sand dunes, and pristine beaches.

The Urros de Liencres, a series of striking, jagged rock formations rising from the sea, are particularly notable. Hiking through Costa Quebrada provides unparalleled views of these geological marvels, along with the opportunity to explore extensive dune fields and hidden coves. The park is a haven for both casual walkers and avid hikers, offering trails that reveal the area's natural splendour from various vantage points.

5. SUANCES PENINSULA

The Suances Peninsula offers some of the most breathtaking coastal views in Cantabria. At the tip of the peninsula stands a historic lighthouse that provides panoramic vistas of both the Playa de la Concha to the west and the dramatic Cantabrian cliffs to the east.

The lighthouse area is ideal for a leisurely walk or a more strenuous hike, with trails that offer spectacular views of the surrounding coastline. The contrast between the serene beach and the rugged cliffs makes Suances a picturesque destination, perfect for those looking to experience both calm and dramatic coastal landscapes.

URRO DEL MANZANO

6. OYAMBRE NATURAL PARK

Located just west of San Vicente de la Barquera, this

park offers a diverse and captivating landscape that combines dunes, marshes and coastal cliffs, as well as stunning views of the Picos de Europa, which rise majestically in the background.

The park's extensive network of trails takes visitors through varied terrains, including sandy beaches, lush marshlands and rocky outcrops. The combination of coastal and mountain scenery makes Oyambre a unique destination, where visitors can enjoy birdwatching, hiking, and exploring secluded beaches.

7. EL SOPLAO CAVE

Located a short drive away from the coast, near San Vicente de la Barquera, El Soplao Cave is famous for its stunning formations of stalactites, stalagmites and unique helictites. The cave's otherworldly beauty, coupled with its fascinating geological features, makes it a must-visit for those interested in exploring Cantabria's subterranean wonders.

8. TINA MENOR ESTUARY

At the western edge of Cantabria, the area around Pechón and the Tina Menor Estuary presents a more rugged and secluded coastline. This region is known for its dramatic cliffs, hidden coves and the tranquil beauty of the estuary, which is surrounded by a network of trails that lead to picturesque spots, perfect for those seeking a quiet retreat.

The natural landscape here remains relatively untouched, offering a sense of isolation and tranquillity. The small town of Pechón adds charm to the area, providing a quaint base for exploring the rugged landscape.

↰ FARO DE LA ISLA DE MOURO

FIELDS IN LIENCRES ↳

PUENTE DEL DIABLO - SANTANDER

SAN VICENTE DE LA BARQUERA

PLAYA DE LAREDO

↲ ERMITA DE LA VIRGEN DEL MAR

PLAYA DE ORIÑÓN ↳

↰ COSTA QUEBRADA

SAN VINCENTE DE LA BARQUERA ↘

UNIVERSIDAD PONTIFICIA DE COMILLAS

Stage 49

BARAKALDO > COLINDRES

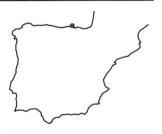

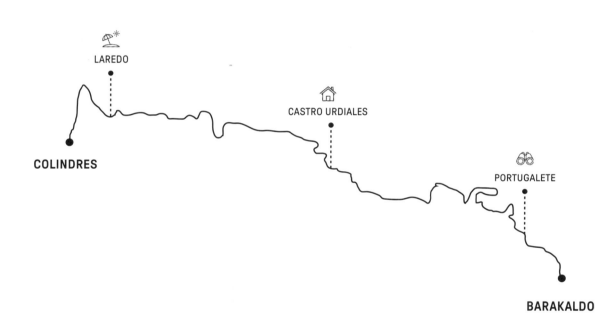

DATE	02/05/2022
DISTANCE	74.59 KM
ELEVATION	2,465 M
TOTAL TIME	10H52
MOVING TIME	10H39

SHOREHOLDER
Jelle Jacobs

STAGE HIGHLIGHTS

 Castro Urdiales
Beautiful medieval town with the Santa Ana Castle and Iglesia de Santa María.

 Bilbao
Vibrant cultural hub, famed for the iconic Guggenheim Museum and its dynamic blend of modern art, rich history, and lively urban charm.

 Vizcaya Bridge, Portugalete
The world's oldest transporter bridge, spanning the Nervión River, designed by Alberto Palacio, a disciple of Eiffel.

 Vía Verde Paseo Itsaslur & del Piquillo
Stunning cliffside walk with breathtaking ocean views.

 Cargadero de Dícido
A mysterious, abandoned loading dock and its charming waterfall.

 Between Sonabia and Laredo
Stunning coastal hike.

 Playa La Salvé de Laredo
A 5 km sandy beach, perfect for surf lovers.

STAGE STORY

All great ideas start with coffee, a cookie, and a good book. For Jelle, Stage 49 began while flipping through the first book of Follow The Coast over a flat white. A chance meeting with the Follow the Coast team planted the seed. Shortly after, the book landed in his hands as a birthday gift, and with it came a challenge: Stage 49 would be his. At the same celebration, Jelle turned to his friend and neighbour Bert. "100 kilometres? I'm in." As they toasted with a Duvel or two, their casual idea turned into a full-fledged plan.

Preparation followed, blending growing fitness, friendship, and a commitment to see the madness through. Self-proclaimed as "the least professional ultrarunners in the world," Jelle and Bert swapped hesitation for all-in determination.

Their adventure began theatrically at a suspension bridge, fuelled by espresso, pastries, and a dramatic reading of its Wikipedia page. The duo quickly transitioned from urban landscapes to the industrial sprawl of the harbour. Along the way, support flowed seamlessly. From a bright yellow rental Peugeot, Marijke and Anne delivered water, sports drinks, nuts, dates, and gingerbread via WhatsApp orders. Meanwhile, Gert-Jan and Max trailed them closely in their West Flemish van, ensuring nothing was left to chance.

The kilometres grew harder. Long stretches inaccessible by car left the runners battling alone. Thorn bushes and barbed wire carved lines across their legs. At times, the path was more an idea than a reality—moments of hopeless frustration gave way to awe at the untamed beauty of the cliffs and the ever-wild Atlantic Ocean on their right.

Around kilometre 60, they conquered both the highest and deepest point of the stage. Exhausted but resolute, Max stepped in to pace the trickiest downhill section after a vital water stop. It's strange how something as simple as cold water can feel like magic.

The final stretch was a test of will. On a long expanse of beach, waves of exhaustion and invincibility alternated. When one faltered, the other offered encouragement. Step by step, they reached the finish line together. Magical doesn't begin to describe it.

The next day, as coffee brewed and sore legs groaned with every descent, Bert and Jelle exchanged grins through the aches. "It was worth it," they said, over and over. And indeed, it was.

Stage 50

COLINDRES > SANTANDER

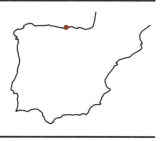

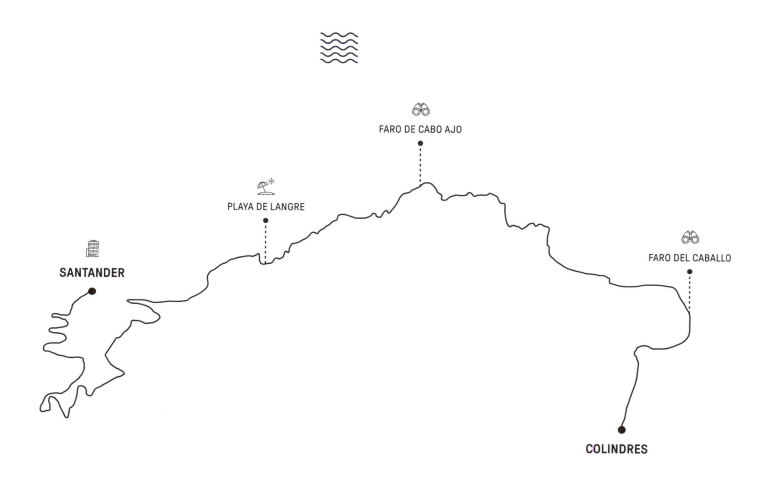

DATE	02/05/2022
DISTANCE	96.22 KM
ELEVATION	2,341 M
TOTAL TIME	11H45
MOVING TIME	11H03

SHOREHOLDERS
Koen Wilssens
Jeremy Genar

STAGE HIGHLIGHTS

 Santander
A lively city known for its beautiful bay, historic landmarks, and coastal charm. This stage captures the essence of the Cantabrian coastline, blending serene beaches with rugged landscapes and vibrant culture.

 Faro del Caballo
An isolated lighthouse accessible via a steep descent of 764 steps down to sea level. The hike rewards you with stunning ocean views and is an absolute must-see.

 Faro de Cabo Ajo
A vibrant, colourful lighthouse standing out against the rugged coastline, offering a perfect spot for photography.

Playa de Langre
A tranquil beach set against dramatic cliffs, perfect for relaxing or admiring the natural surroundings.

STAGE STORY

When we planned to run a Follow The Coast stage, neither of us had gone beyond 60 km. With injuries hampering preparation, we still knew—no matter what—we'd finish our 100 km!

Jeremy planned Stage 50 well in advance. Mapping the best coastal tracks from Laredo to Santander was half the fun. We agreed not to run fast for the first 15 kilometres—long asphalt roads around a bay made it easy to overdo it early. Pacing wasn't our strength, but resisting our instincts proved the right call.

After 15 kilometres, we reached Santoña. Behind the village lay a stunning nature reserve, with Faro del Caballo as a highlight. We nearly descended the entire 200m cliff for a photo but, sensing what lay ahead, I skipped the final steps. Climbing back up, we pressed on.

The first marathon felt smooth. By noon, starting at 5 am meant we already had serious mileage behind us. The scenery and conversation made time fly. At 50 km, our halfway stop, we felt euphoric—legs fresh, spirits high, nothing could stop us!

From 50 to 80 km, time melted away. Coastal single tracks stretched for 20 km, alternating between cliff tops and sandy beaches. Running on empty beaches was surreal—I never knew Spain had such hidden gems.

We took it 10 km at a time, motivating each other. But after 80 km, my legs betrayed me. Cramping badly, I couldn't run five steps without seizing up. Scenery? Who cared—I just wanted to finish and never walk again. Koen still felt strong and pulled me through the final half marathon, promising eternal Follow The Coast glory.

For Koen, the last 15 kilometres were hilarious. My cramps became a running joke—literally. At one point, I cramped on my left leg, and laughing at it made my right leg seize too. The last 7 kilometres, joined by Max & Gert-Jan, felt endless. When Koen suggested, "Jeremy, let's run for the final pictures," my tendons staged a full rebellion.

At the finish, the long-awaited ice cream van appeared—the perfect reward. Gert-Jan captured us on a bench, savouring that simple joy.

That night in the hotel, we laughed about my cramps—especially how I hobbled to the plane. Three months of rest followed, perfect for reminiscing. As always with these things, "never again" quickly turned into "which stage is next?"

Stage 51

SANTANDER > PLAYA DE LA TABLÍA

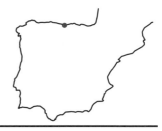

FARO CABO MAYOR

ISLA DE LA VIRGEN DEL MAR

FARO DE SUANCES

URROS DE LIENCRES

SANTANDER

PLAYA DE LA TABLÍA

ISLA DE LA VIRGEN DE LA MAR

STAGE HIGHLIGHTS

 Santander
A lively city known for its beautiful bay, historic landmarks, and coastal charm. This stage captures the essence of the Cantabrian coastline, blending serene beaches with rugged landscapes and vibrant culture.

 Faro Cabo Mayor
Dramatic lighthouse dominating a cliff.

Isla de la Virgen de la Mar
Island connected to the mainland with a bridge, featuring a chapel honouring the Virgin of the Sea.

 Urros de Liencres
Sharp rock formations sticking out from the sea, creating a dramatic landscape.

 Faro de Suances
Lighthouse with panoramic view on Playa de la Concha on the west and rugged Cantabrian cliffs to the east.

Stage 52

PLAYA DE LA TABLÍA > PUERTAS DE VIDIAGO

STAGE HIGHLIGHTS

⌂ **Comillas**
Charming town of boasting an array of architectural marvels, including Palacio Sobrellano, the House of the Duke of Almodóvar, and the unique El Capricho, designed by Gaudí. It is also home to Ciesu University, the Pantheon of the Marquess of Comillas, and Casa Ocejo, each bearing witness to Comillas' royal history.

⌂ **San Vicente de la Barquera**
A picturesque village crowned by the 13th- century Castillo del Rey.

👀 **Molino el Bolao**
An abandoned mill with a small waterfall where a stream flows into the sea—a hidden gem in this scenic area.

👀 **Ruinas de la Iglesia de Santa María de Tina**
An abandoned monastery near Puertas de Vidiago.

↱ Regions 3 / 10
   Asturias

10,604 km²
1,010,000 inhabitants

→ VILLAVICIOSA

CADAVÉU - VALDÉS

↳ Asturias is a hidden gem for adventurers, offering a perfect mix of wild coastlines and towering mountains. The region's coast features golden beaches, rugged cliffs, and secluded bays, perfect for surfing and exploring. Inland, the Picos de Europa mountains rise to 2,650 m, providing a playground for hikers, mountain bikers, and ski tourers.

As part of Spain's Green Belt, Asturias is home to preserved nature and wildlife like the Cantabrian brown bear and Iberian wolf. Its low population density helps maintain its natural charm. The coastal cities of Gijón and Avilés show the industrial side, with Avilés hosting the Oscar Niemeyer Cultural Centre. Yet, the unspoiled beaches, like Playa del Silencio and Playa de Torimbia, truly capture Asturias' magic. With mild winters, cool summers, and abundant rainfall, Asturias nurtures lush vegetation and diverse ecosystems, making it a haven for hikers, birdwatchers, and nature lovers.

Additionally, the Asturian culture is reflected in its traditional music, dance, and cuisine, with local dishes like fabada asturiana (a rich bean stew) and sidra (cider) being staples in the region. The people of Asturias take great pride in their identity, making it a culturally vibrant and welcoming destination for travellers.

Asturias

400 km Coastline
Capital: Oviedo

Asturias
↳ Introduction

HOW TO GET THERE

Asturias is well connected, with its primary transportation hub located in the capital, Oviedo. Asturias Airport (OVD), situated around 40 km from Oviedo, provides flights to national and European destinations, making it a convenient entry point for travellers.

For those preferring to travel by train, Oviedo Railway Station offers national connections, though there are no direct international routes. The region is also accessible by bus, with extensive services linking major cities like Gijón and Avilés.

WHERE TO STAY

Asturias' diverse landscape offers a variety of places to stay, each providing unique experiences that showcase the region's natural beauty and cultural heritage.

As the capital, Oviedo is a charming city known for its rich history, medieval architecture and lively atmosphere. Visitors can explore landmarks like Oviedo Cathedral and the Pre-Romanesque Church of San Julián de los Prados, both UNESCO World Heritage Sites. The city's vibrant street life and excellent food scene make it a great base for exploring the region.

Asturias' largest city, Gijón is a coastal destination with a perfect blend of urban excitement and beach relaxation. The city's lively promenade, Playa de San Lorenzo, and historic neighbourhood, Cimavilla, offer plenty to explore. With its maritime heritage and cultural festivals, Gijón is an ideal destination for travellers seeking both beach and culture.

The quaint fishing village of Cudillero is one of Asturias' most picturesque spots. Nestled between cliffs, its brightly coloured houses overlook a charming harbour. Cudillero's seafood restaurants and stunning coastal views make it a perfect retreat for those looking to unwind.

A coastal town surrounded by the Picos de Europa mountains, Llanes offers a blend of natural beauty and history. Its medieval old town and nearby beaches, such as Playa de Torimbia, are ideal for visitors looking to explore both land and sea.

Famous for its prehistoric cave paintings at Tito Bustillo Cave, Ribadesella is another attractive coastal town. Its river estuary and long sandy beaches make it popular among nature lovers and history enthusiasts alike.

HISTORY

Asturias is not just about natural beauty; it also has a rich cultural and historical heritage dating back to prehistoric times. The region is dotted with ancient Romanesque churches, palaces and castles that speak to its storied past. Notable sites include the historic town of Oviedo, with its UNESCO World Heritage Sites, and the archaeological remains of prehistoric caves adorned with ancient rock art, including the Cave of Altamira, home to some of the world's most important prehistoric cave art.

The Kingdom of Asturias was a crucial player during the early stages of the Reconquista, becoming a bastion of Christian resistance to Muslim rule in the 8th century. Asturias is also known for its Pre-Romanesque architecture, a unique style developed during the early Middle Ages. Today, the region preserves this heritage while embracing modern life, offering visitors a window into Spain's past alongside contemporary attractions.

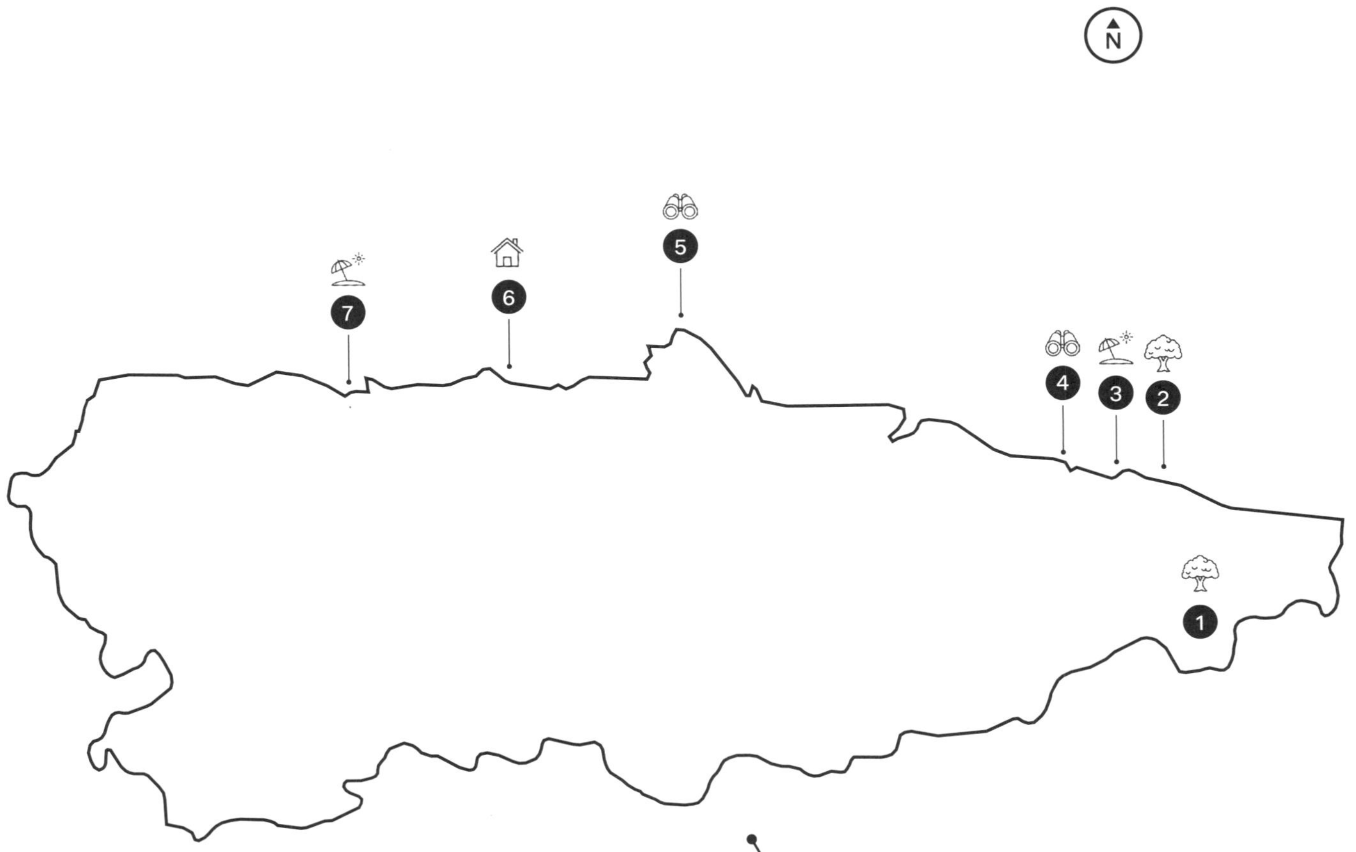

ASTURIAS

SPAIN

EXPLORE / HIGHLIGHTS

1. Picos de Europa
2. Senda Costera
3. Playa de Torimbia
4. Bufones de Pría
5. Cabo de Peñas
6. Cudillero
7. Playa del Silencio

REGION 3 / 10

FARO DE AVILES, PENINSULA DE SAN JUAN

Asturias
↳ Highlights

Boasting a dramatic coastline where rugged cliffs meet secluded beaches and striking rock formations, Asturias' scenic landscapes make it one of the most captivating regions in Spain.

1. PICOS DE EUROPA

Though not directly on the coast, the Picos de Europa mountains provide a striking inland backdrop to Asturias' coastal beauty. This stunning national park features peaks over 2,600 metres, deep gorges, and diverse wildlife.

A paradise for hikers, the park's numerous trails offer breathtaking views of both the mountains and the sea. The Lakes of Covadonga, located within the park, provide a serene setting, ideal for picnicking and relaxation.

2. SENDA COSTERA

The Senda Costera (Coastal Path) is one of Asturias' most scenic hiking trails, running along the rugged coastline. The path passes by dramatic cliffs, hidden beaches, and charming villages, offering panoramic sea views. Varying in difficulty, it caters to both casual walkers and seasoned hikers. Along the way, you may spot seabirds, coastal flora, and breathtaking rock formations shaped by the sea over centuries.

3. PLAYA DE TORIMBIA

Located near Llanes, Playa de Torimbia is one of Asturias' most picturesque beaches. Enclosed by towering cliffs, this crescent-shaped beach is known for its fine sands and clear waters, making it a favourite for beachgoers and surfers.

Its remote location and unspoiled natural beauty offer a peaceful retreat, while the views from the cliffs above provide a stunning vantage point of the sweeping coastline.

4. BUFONES DE PRÍA

A must-see natural spectacle, the Bufones de Pría are powerful sea geysers created when waves crash against the cliffs, sending water surging through rock fissures. This dramatic display is especially striking during high tide. The surrounding coastline, with its rugged cliffs and picturesque hiking trails, makes it an ideal destination for adventurers eager to witness nature's raw power.

5. CABO DE PEÑAS

The northernmost point of Asturias, Cabo de Peñas is one of the region's most iconic landmarks. This rocky cape features sweeping views of the Cantabrian Sea, rugged cliffs, and a historic lighthouse that has guided sailors for centuries.

Hiking trails around the area provide stunning panoramic views, while the dramatic landscape, accompanied by the sounds of crashing waves, creates a serene and adventurous atmosphere.

6. CUDILLERO

Nestled between steep cliffs, Cudillero is a charming fishing village known for its colourful houses cascading down to the harbour. Its picturesque streets and lively atmosphere make it a must-visit destination. Cudillero is renowned for its seafood restaurants, where freshly caught fish is served daily. Its proximity to beautiful beaches and scenic coastal paths makes it an excellent base for exploring Asturias' coastline.

7. PLAYA DEL SILENCIO

A hidden gem on the Asturian coast, Playa del Silencio is a pristine beach surrounded by towering cliffs and crystal-clear waters.

Known for its unspoiled beauty, this secluded beach offers a peaceful escape from crowded tourist spots. It's ideal for surfers and nature lovers, while its golden-hour scenery makes it a favourite for photographers and romantic getaways.

CENTRO NIEMEYER, AVILES

ERMITA DE LA REGALINA, VALDES

ERMITA DE LA REGALINA, VALDES

Stage 53

PUERTAS DE VIDIAGO > SANTA MERA

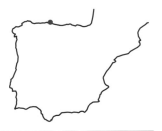

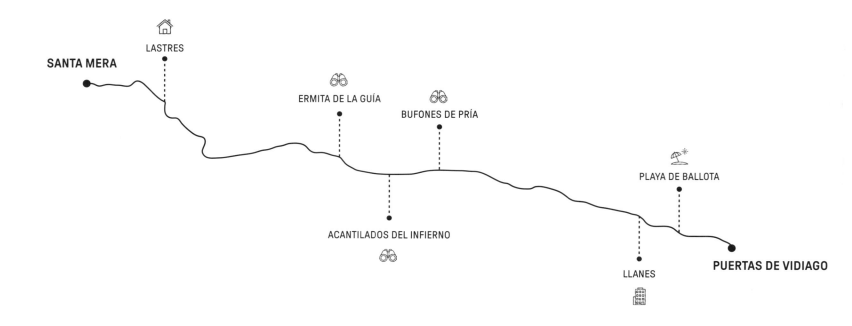

DATE	06/05/2022
DISTANCE	98.20 KM
ELEVATION	3100 M
TOTAL TIME	13H24
MOVING TIME	13H24

SHOREHOLDERS
Maarten Hermans
Sander Donders

STAGE HIGHLIGHTS

Llanes
Vibrant coastal city, boasting a plethora of beautiful beaches, including the picturesque Playa de Torimbia. Surrounding cliffs offer breathtaking vistas of the snow-capped Picos de Europa.

Lastres
Charming fishing village enchanting visitors with its hillside views and coastal charm.

Bufones de Santiuste en Arenillas
Striking feature where unique rock formations create natural geysers, sending water shooting skyward as waves crash against them.

Playa de Ballota
Beach with azure waters and cliffs with views of the Picos de Europa.

Scenic route between Llanes and Ribadesella
Features countless beaches, along with Bufones de Pría and the dramatic Acantilados del Infierno.

Ermita de La Guía, Ribadesella
Chapel dating back to the 16th century.

STAGE STORY

After Maarten called me with the idea to run a 100 km race, I was terrified. The longest I had ever run was just under a half marathon. I asked, "Why not start with a full marathon?" but Maarten responded, "Let's make it a real challenge." A few beers later, I was convinced, and we signed up to tackle the Spanish coastline together.

Training was intense. We gradually increased our distances—first 42 km, then 70 km, and even tackled some "hilly trails." We felt ready, but then COVID hit and forced us to postpone. I remember feeling uneasy, thinking we were only at about 70% of our original strength when we finally returned to training. It made me nervous.

The night before the race, excitement mixed with anxiety. I thought, "This is the biggest athletic challenge I've ever faced." We had food packed and the trail mapped out, but I kept my expectations low. I was prepared for a DNF (did not finish), especially after experiencing nightmares about running through muddy streams and ending up with wet feet for the entire race.

Race day arrived, and we were pumped but still a bit jittery. We started off strong, maybe too strong, running up and down hills. By the 5 km mark, my fears materialised—water, mud, and cow dung up to our knees! "Great fun," I thought, but there was no turning back. We pressed on, and the first half of the race went smoothly. However, by the 50 km mark, we felt the toll of the terrain.

Maarten noted, "As Dutchmen used to flat landscapes, the hills and heat of Spain were brutal." Our running turned into striding, and eventually, we were walking. "Every flat stretch in the shade felt like a blessing," I added, but at 70 km, I was nauseous, and chafing became a serious issue. It was hard, really hard.

At 80 km, I was deep in struggle mode, and Maarten pulled me through those final kilometres. We started to have some hallucinations, unable to eat anything, which was bizarre but oddly fascinating. Yet as the finish line drew closer, our spirits lifted. The sight of the lukewarm Duvel waiting for us reignited our energy, and we found the strength for a final sprint.

This experience taught me about my limits. "It's a story that will be shared in pubs for years to come," I said, and Maarten nodded in agreement. After crossing that finish line, if you'd asked us whether we'd run an ultramarathon again, we probably would have said no. Yet here we are, already cautiously considering when to embark on our next adventure.

Stage 54

SANTA MERA > BAÑUGUES

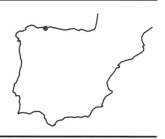

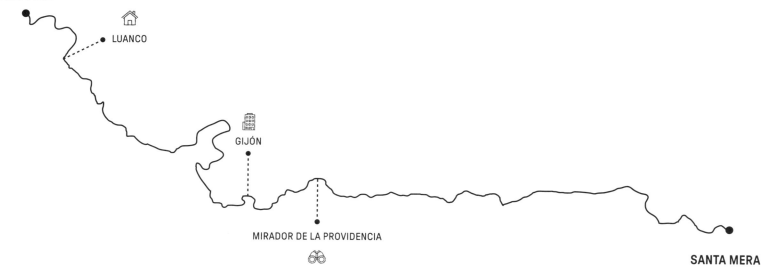

DATE	07/05/2022
DISTANCE	88 KM
ELEVATION	1,850 M
TOTAL TIME	16H30
MOVING TIME	15H00

SHOREHOLDERS
Stéphanie Cobbaert
Federico Fiz

STAGE HIGHLIGHTS

Villaviciosa
Charming village nestled on the estuary of the Villaviciosa River, just 5 km from the coast, known for its cider and welcoming atmosphere.

Gijón
Largest city in Asturias. Santa Catalina hill with Eduardo Chillida's Elogio del Horizonte set atop old military fortifications. The historic centre is located on a peninsula, featuring the Palacio de Revillagigedo, City Hall, and the San Pedro Church. West of the city, the Campa Torres offers a mix of Roman archaeological remains and panoramic views of the port.

Luanco
A picturesque town with colonial-style houses and the Santa María de Luanco church perched dramatically by the sea.

Mirador de La Providencia
Providing an impressive view over the city, this viewpoint symbolises the bow of a ship jutting out from the hillside, with contemporary art installations dotting the site.

STAGE STORY

I wasn't supposed to run that day. It's all Bert's fault. My lovely brother-in-law had planned to run this stage with Stéphanie, my wife, but when the run got postponed due to COVID, Bert bailed. 100% his fault. Well, 50%. The other 50%? Steph's stubbornness.

For months, she'd been threatening to run the stage solo. At first, I dismissed it as a passing idea—she wasn't training. Sure, we live in Mallorca with plenty of opportunities to run in the Tramuntana mountains, but Steph wasn't exactly taking advantage of them.

Fast forward to three days before D-Day. Steph looked me in the eyes and said: "Fede, I'm running this stage on Saturday. It would be nice if you came to support me. But I'm going, no matter what."

In 72 hours, we went from "this won't happen" to scrambling to book flights, reserve hotels, buy gels, and gather supplies. Naturally, I teased her into buying a thermal blanket, declaring it a must-have for all "professional ultrarunners."

The night before, we boarded our flight to Oviedo with a backpack full of doubts, backup plans, far too many gels, and a kilo of Mallorquín ensaimada for Max that we—predictably—ate ourselves. By 7 am, we met Max at the starting line with +1,800 m of climbing and 100 km ahead of us. What could go wrong?

The day was cold but sunny, the path daunting but beautiful. The run became a series of moments: half spent mindlessly moving forward, others consumed by a desperate urge to quit. And then there were the moments that made it all worthwhile—supporting, complimenting, and balancing each other when the doubts grew too loud.

The night brought cooler temperatures and tougher hills. We were undertrained, unprepared, and wildly out of our depth. But we had each other. And sometimes, that's all you need.

In the end, belief and logic blurred together, carrying us across the finish line as a team. Alone, we wouldn't have made it to the start.

"When the snow falls and the white winds blow, the lone wolf dies, but the pack survives."

Stage 55

BAÑUGUES > CASTAÑERAS

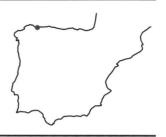

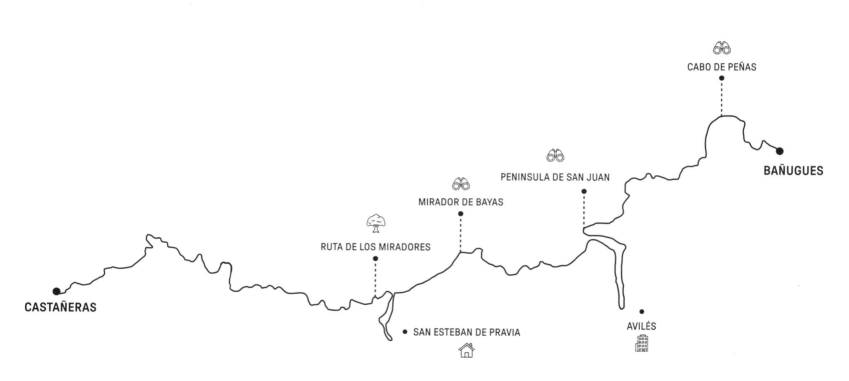

DATE	08/05/2022
DISTANCE	103.5 KM
ELEVATION	2,659 M
TOTAL TIME	17H04
MOVING TIME	14H29

SHOREHOLDER
Sander De Deckere

STAGE HIGHLIGHTS

Avilés
Don't miss the Centro Oscar Niemeyer, an iconic cultural hub. The Philippe Cousteau Anchor Museum in nearby Salinas is dedicated to maritime history.

San Esteban de Pravia
Charming village nestled in the Bay of Nalon, home to the historic Cargadero de Carbón.

Cabo Peñas
Some of Asturias' highest and wildest cliffs crowned by a unique lighthouse.

The Ruta de los Miradores
Must-do coastal hike, starting with a 124 m staircase; leading you over lush green bays and cliffs.

Peninsula de San Juan
Offers striking views of Avilés.

STAGE STORY

Spain, Bañugues, Sunday, May 8. After two years of delays and switching stages, it was finally time for my Follow the Coast stage, a 100 km relay along Europe's stunning coastline.

Despite setbacks—like a muscle tear in February and my wedding last month—I couldn't skip it, as I had already used my pass for the Paris Marathon. I mapped my own route, staying as close to the sea as possible, though it ended up with more elevation than I'd hoped for.

The race started at 7.05 am, and the first few kilometres were rough, as I got lost on a dead-end trail. Soon enough, though, the rising sun revealed the stunning beauty of the coastline. By kilometre 13, I had finished my first peninsula, amazed by the scenery, and at 25 km, I reached Playa de Xagó to refuel and prepare for the next 75 km.

The middle stretch took me past dramatic cliffs, rock formations, and eucalyptus forests, offering much-needed shade. Around kilometre 55, I began to struggle, but Maximilien joined me on his gravel bike, cheering me on with conversation and even offering a cheese sandwich, which felt like a lifesaver. After a quick coffee stop in San Esteban, I felt recharged and ready to push on.

By kilometre 80, I had reached a personal distance record. The final section followed the Camino de Santiago, with 700 meters of climbing on increasingly dark and difficult trails. The pain in my Achilles and knee intensified, but knowing I was nearing the end kept me going.

In the final kilometres, with my wife cheering me on, I found the strength for a last push. I crossed the finish line at 12:10 AM, celebrating with an ice-cold Duvel beer, making it an unforgettable day.

Stage 56

CASTAÑERAS > SAN ANTONIO

STAGE HIGHLIGHTS

Luarca
Charming fishing town with a picturesque harbour. The peninsula features a lighthouse, chapel, and a cliffside cemetery.

Playa del Silencio
This tranquil, beautiful beach is framed by towering cliffs and a small rocky peninsula.

Ermita de la Regalina
Small chapel perched on a high cliff, offering breathtaking views of the coastline. An iconic pilgrimage site, especially during the Fiesta de La Regalina, a traditional Asturian celebration.

Cabo de San Agustín
Two lighthouses stand watch over the sea.

Punta de la Atalaya
Sweeping views of the Atlantic and the rugged Asturian coast.

↱ Regions 4 / 10
Galicia

29,574.42 km²
2,701,000 inhabitants

→ FARO DE CABO HOME

SANTUÁRIO DE SANTO ANDRÉ DE TEIXIDO

↳ Galicia, located in the northwest corner of Spain, is a captivating region of dramatic contrasts where the wild Atlantic Ocean meets lush, green landscapes, earning it the nickname "Green Spain." With over 1,500 km of intricate coastline featuring rugged cliffs, pristine beaches, and serene estuaries, Galicia offers an ever-changing seascape that appeals to nature lovers and outdoor enthusiasts alike.

Its oceanic climate, characterised by mild winters and cool summers with abundant rainfall, nurtures vibrant ecosystems and lush vegetation. Rolling meadows, evergreen oak and chestnut forests, and coastal flora like sea daffodils and sand lilies thrive in this fertile land. Inland, the terrain transitions to thick forests and rugged mountains, while the diverse coastal plant life supports an array of birds and marine species. This unique blend of temperate and coastal environments makes Galicia an ideal destination for hikers, birdwatchers, and those seeking a deep connection with nature.

Galicia

1,500 km Coastline
Capital: Santiago de Compostela

Galicia
↳ Introduction

HOW TO GET AROUND

Galicia is easily accessible, with several main transport hubs. The largest gateway is Santiago de Compostela Airport (SCQ), located about 10 kilometres from the city centre. This airport connects Galicia to numerous European destinations and major Spanish cities, making it a convenient choice for travellers. The region's second-largest airport, A Coruña Airport (LCG), offers connections to Spanish cities and some international routes, while Vigo Airport (VGO) provides flights primarily to Spanish hubs, with a few select international routes.

For those travelling by rail, Santiago de Compostela and Vigo-Guixar Railway Stations are the region's busiest. These stations link Galicia with key Spanish cities like Madrid and Barcelona, and Vigo-Guixar additionally offers connections to Portugal. Notably, Galicia is a significant stop on the Camino de Santiago pilgrimage, a network of European walking and cycling routes leading to Santiago de Compostela.

WHERE TO STAY

Though located inland, Santiago de Compostela serves as an ideal base for excursions along the nearby coast. Its historical centre, recognised as a UNESCO World Heritage site, captures the essence of medieval Spain with narrow, cobbled streets and grand squares. The iconic Cathedral of Santiago, the final stop of the Camino de Santiago de Compostela, attracts millions of visitors annually. Santiago's thriving university scene and range of cozy cafes, tapas bars and artisanal shops make it a bustling yet relaxed destination for all travellers.

Moving closer to the coast, A Coruña is an excellent choice for those who seek both urban energy and beachside leisure. Known for its Roman lighthouse, glazed balconies and long seaside promenade, the city is very busy in August, during the María Pita festivities.

In the south, Vigo is Galicia's largest city and a lively port hub, celebrated for its rich maritime heritage and access to the beautiful Cíes Islands, which are part of the Atlantic Islands of Galicia National Park. These islands have earned a reputation as one of Europe's most scenic beach destinations.

For those seeking a classic beach escape, Sanxenxo stands out. Often called the "summer capital" of Galicia, it attracts the crowds with its numerous beaches, where visitors can enjoy sunbathing, sailing and other activities.

Further south, the historic town of Baiona, in the province of Pontevedra, combines history and natural beauty, with the impressive Monterreal Fortress overlooking the town and harbour and scenic beaches that make it a peaceful retreat for history enthusiasts and nature lovers alike.

HISTORY

Galicia's history is a rich blend of Celtic, Roman and medieval influences, shaping its unique cultural identity. The ancient Gallaeci Celts first settled here, leaving behind the iconic stone castros (fortified villages) scattered across the rugged landscape. Roman rule brought infrastructure and trade, with landmarks like the nearly 2,000-year-old Tower of Hercules in A Coruña – the oldest working Roman lighthouse in the world.

In the Middle Ages, the rise of the Camino de Santiago pilgrimage made Galicia a major Christian destination, attracting pilgrims from all over Europe to Santiago de Compostela, believed to house St. James's remains. This pilgrimage fostered a unique exchange of architectural styles and traditions, enriching Galicia's cultural tapestry.

Today, Galicia celebrates its deep maritime heritage, with Gallegos honouring their Celtic roots through music, language, and festivals tied to land and sea. Its lighthouses, fishing villages, and coastal fortresses offer travellers a glimpse into a region where history and modern life coexist, making Galicia a unique destination in Spain.

GALICIA

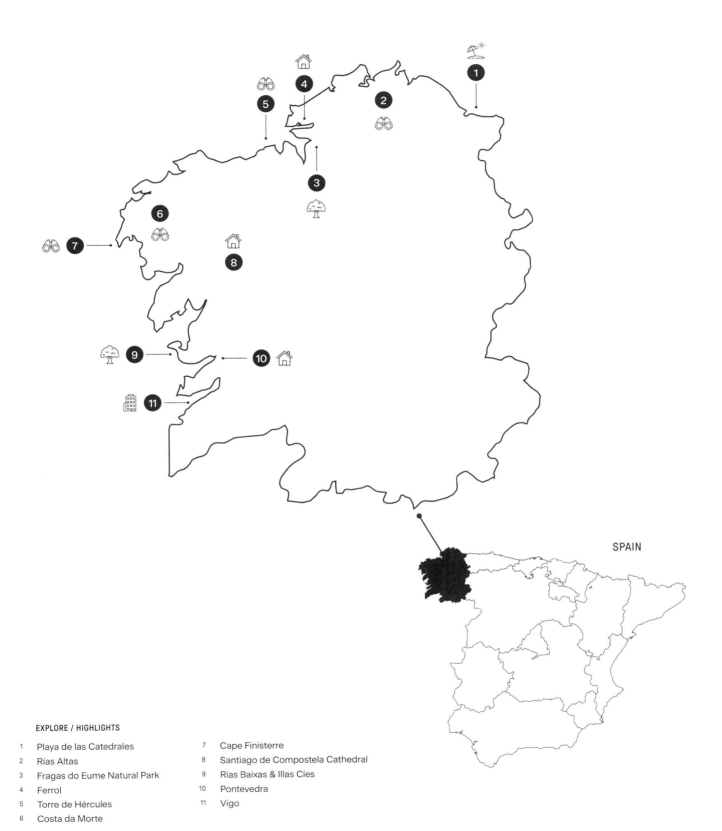

EXPLORE / HIGHLIGHTS

1. Playa de las Catedrales
2. Rías Altas
3. Fragas do Eume Natural Park
4. Ferrol
5. Torre de Hércules
6. Costa da Morte
7. Cape Finisterre
8. Santiago de Compostela Cathedral
9. Rías Baixas & Illas Cíes
10. Pontevedra
11. Vigo

PLAYA DE LAS CATEDRALES

Galicia
↳ Highlights

Galicia's coastline, often called "Godlike Galicia," is a wild stretch where Spain's green, rugged cliffs meet the fierce Atlantic. To the north, the Rías Altas create a jagged landscape of deep bays, dramatic capes, and Europe's tallest cliffs, rising 620 meters above sea level. Moving westward, the Costa da Morte – named for its shipwreck history – extends from A Coruña to Cape Finisterre, winding through hidden beaches, remote coves, and small islands that feel lost to time.

Further south, the Rías Baixas region offers a gentler, almost "tropical" climate, home to Galicia's famed Albariño vineyards and the lively harbour towns of Vigo and Pontevedra. This coastline is also spiritually significant as part of the Camino de Santiago pilgrimage, ending at Santiago de Compostela and extending to Finisterre, the "end of the world."

1. PLAYA DE LAS CATEDRALES

A must-visit natural wonder, Playa de las Catedrales is known for its towering rock arches and caves that appear at low tide. It offers a mystical experience as visitors wander beneath natural stone arches that resemble cathedral aisles.

The nearby town of Laxe and its long, white-sand beach is set against the backdrop of dramatic cliffs, while the fishing village of Muxía is known for its Santuario da Virxe da Barca, a shrine perched on the rocks and surrounded by powerful waves.

2. RÍAS ALTAS

Streching from Ribadeo to A Coruña, the Rías Altas, or "Upper Rias", are marked by steep cliffs, secluded beaches and dramatic capes. Along this rugged coast lies the famed Serra da Capelada, a range known for its untouched landscapes and striking views, and Cabo Ortegal, a rocky cape and lighthouse that provides a breathtaking vantage point of the Atlantic.

More panoramic views of Galicia's coastline are found just to the south, at Vixía Herbeira, where the towering sea cliffs rise up to 620 m (the highest in continental Europe), creating a sensation of being on the edge of the world. This area is home to diverse bird species and is ideal for scenic walks along cliffside trails. Nearby, the small village of San Andrés de Teixido is known for its pilgrimage traditions and its charming stone church, set against a stunning coastal backdrop.

3. FRAGAS DO EUME NATURAL PARK

Located near the town of Pontedeume, this lush, ancient forest – one of the best-preserved Atlantic coastal forests in Europe – is threaded with hiking trails and the Eume River, offering visitors a unique glimpse into Galicia's biodiversity.

4. FERROL

Surrounded by beautiful countryside but often overlooked, Ferrol is known for its historic shipyards and maritime heritage, which you can explore at the Museo Naval. You can also sample authentic seafood dishes, and walk up to the 16th-century Castillo de San Felipe for great river views.

5. TORRE DE HÉRCULES

When the Romans arrived in the 2nd century BC, they brought trade, infrastructure, and a cultural shift from the Celtic Gallaeci people and their fortified stone settlements. The Tower of Hercules, a Roman lighthouse in A Coruña that has stood for nearly 2,000 years, remains a symbol of this era and is the oldest functioning lighthouse in the world.

PONTECESO, A CORUÑA

FAROL DE CANDIEIRA

6. COSTA DA MORTE

Southwest of the Rías Altas is the Costa da Morte ("the coast of death"), named after the many shipwrecks that have occurred along its treacherous shores. This coastline stretches from Malpica to Finisterre and is known for its fierce waves, rocky promontories, and hauntingly beautiful seascapes. Here, the interplay of cliffs, beaches, and sea caves provides a stunning, albeit sombre, spectacle.

7. CAPE FINISTERRE

Cape Finisterre is one of Galicia's most iconic locations, historically known as the "end of the world." Pilgrims from the Camino de Santiago often conclude their journey at this windswept cape, where a lighthouse stands as a beacon above the endless Atlantic.

The sunsets at Finisterre are especially mesmerising, offering sweeping views of the ocean from one of the westernmost points of Europe.

8. SANTIAGO DE COMPOSTELA CATHEDRAL

One of the world's most important Christian pilgrimage sites, the beautifully ornate Santiago de Compostela cathedral houses the shrine of Saint James the Apostle, which marks the traditional end to the Camino de Santiago since the early Middle Ages. This pilgrimage has shaped Galicia's cultural identity, bringing millions of visitors annually and fostering a unique blend of spirituality and hospitality.

9. RÍAS BAIXAS & ILLAS CÍES

The Rías Baixas, or "Lower Rias," span from Muros to the Portuguese border and are known for their softer landscapes, protected estuaries, and mild microclimates. This region is famous for its white-sand beaches, vibrant fishing villages, and picturesque islands.

Illas Cíes, an archipelago off the coast of Vigo, is the jewel of the Rías Baixas. Part of the Atlantic Islands of Galicia National Park, these islands feature crystal-clear turquoise waters, fine white sands, and rugged cliffs. Dubbed "the Galician Caribbean," the Cíes Islands offer an array of outdoor activities, from hiking and snorkelling to birdwatching, and are only accessible by ferry during certain months to protect their pristine environment.

10. PONTEVEDRA

Blending coastal charm with historic architecture, Pontevedra features riverside plazas and museums, with the nearby Illa de Ons accessible by ferry. Local landmarks include the Palace of Lourizán, and further inland, the canyons and vineyards of Ribeira Sacra.

11. VIGO

Vigo, Galicia's largest city, serves as a vibrant hub for maritime heritage and culture. The port of Vigo is one of Europe's busiest fishing ports, and the city's old town, known as Casco Vello, provides a rich historical atmosphere with its narrow alleys and bustling markets. The nearby Rande Bridge, crossing the Vigo estuary, offers stunning views and marks the entrance to the scenic Rías Baixas.

FARO DE PUNTA FROUXEIRA

EL BANCO MAS BONITA DEL MUNDA, LOIBA ↘

↳ MIRADOR DO CRUCEIRO

ILLA DE TORALLA, VIGO ↘

↰ FARO DA PUNTA ATALAIA

CASTILLO DE MONTREAL, BAIONA ↳

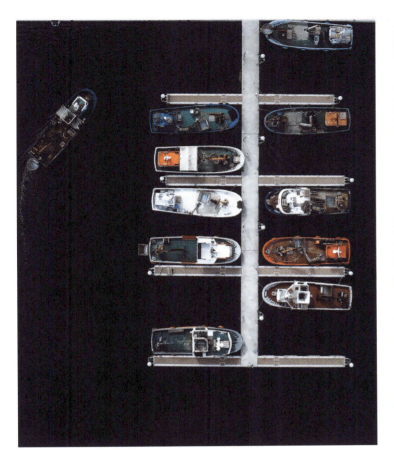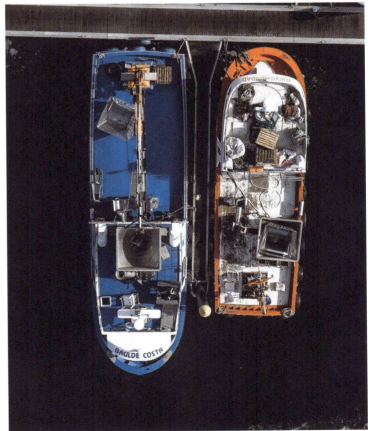

123

↳ FARO RONCADOIRA

ARO DE PUNTA FROUXEIRA ↴

↰ PUNTA ESTACA DE BARES   FARO DE CABO VILÁN ↴

MONUMENTO Á MARIÑA UNIVERSAL, MONTEFERO

↰ FARO DE CABO SILLEIRO

Stage 57

SAN ANTONIO > LAGO

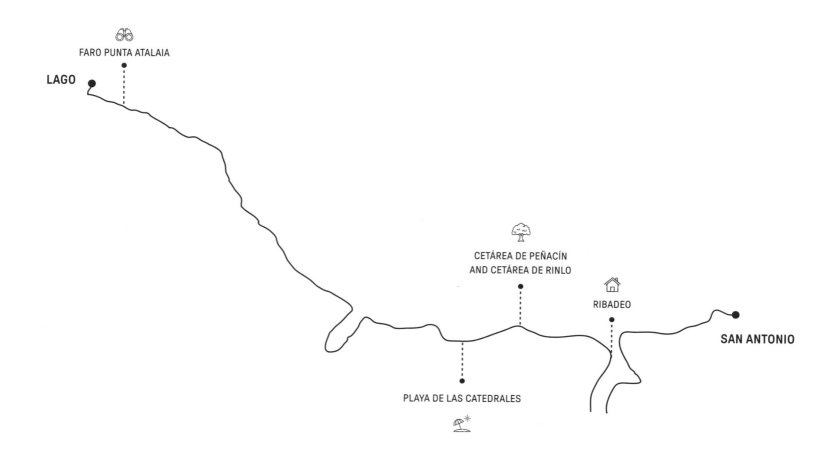

DATE	12/10/2024
DISTANCE	102.47 KM
ELEVATION	1,331 M
TOTAL TIME	15H15
MOVING TIME	14H57

SHOREHOLDER
Milan Cools

PLAYA DE LAS CATEDRALES

STAGE HIGHLIGHTS

 Tapia de Casariego
Village with picturesque harbour and lighthouse on a peninsula.

 Ribadeo
Where the River Eo separates Asturias from Galicia. This vibrant town, just 2 km from the bay, features the scenic Ribadeo Lighthouse.

 Cetárea de Peñacín and Cetárea de Rinlo
Offer excellent hiking opportunities with unique photo spots. These small, abandoned seafood farms dotting the coastline reflect the region's maritime history and charm.

 Playa de las Catedrales
Famous for its rock arches visible at low tide, allowing exploration beneath the arches and into caves.

 Faro Punta Atalaia
Sitting atop dramatic cliffs, this lighthouse provides stunning views of the rugged coastline, a popular spot for photography.

STAGE STORY

We set off for Stage 57 at 7.30 am, starting on a cliff near Tapia de Casariego, illuminated only by my headlamp and a stunning starry sky—my training ground. Surrounded by friends, family, and my girlfriend, I felt a mix of emotions as I prepared for the challenge I'd trained three years to conquer.

The first few kilometres were hilly but manageable. I conserved energy by walking the steep ascents, mindful of the 14-hour run ahead. At kilometre 10, I faced an overgrown path that led me into a farmer's cornfield right as he was harvesting. My feet got wet from morning dew, but I was unconcerned knowing I had an extra pair of shoes in Max's supply van. With the ocean on my right, I caught glimpses of a breathtaking sunrise.

At kilometre 13, I reunited with my support crew in the next village, switched out my favourite (but damp) shoes, and refuelled. The early momentum continued smoothly until about kilometre 30, when I hit a slump. A friend from my support group offered to run alongside me, reminding me that it was normal to feel fatigued after using up my reserves.

In Rinlo, I paused to chat with my loved ones, appreciating their mental boost. Their presence distracted me from my exhaustion, even helping me forget about the rash on my leg. I decided to go commando for the rest of the race. As my group cheered, "First marathon down!" I felt reenergised, knowing I was almost halfway.

But soon, I faced the toughest kilometres. After navigating beautiful cliffs, I entered the dull concrete suburbs of Viladaíde. I knew this section lacked coastal bridges, forcing me to follow the river inland through Lagoa dos Patos.

At kilometre 55, I met my support group again, and Max handed me a refreshing can of Coke instead of the usual powders. Hugging my girlfriend while "Don't Stop Believin'" played in the background provided a much-needed lift. I switched back to my favourite shoes, and at Kilometre 60, I indulged in the legendary Ultra Pancake—two Snickers wrapped in a pancake.

As I approached the finish line at kilometre 102, I saw the silhouettes of my loved ones. Forgetting my pain, I ran across the finish line of Stage 57 after over 15 hours of running, tears still fresh on my cheeks.

October 13, 2024, will forever be etched in my memory. The emotional rollercoaster from Tapia de Casariego to San Cibrao was remarkable, and I realised I never truly ran alone, with my family and friends supporting me every step of the way.

Stage 58

LAGO > O MOSTEIRO

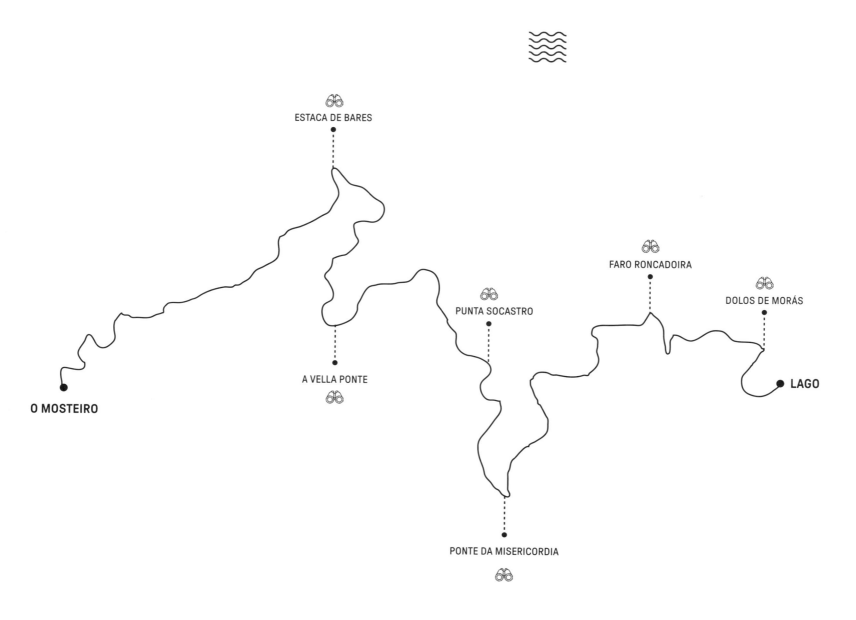

DATE	11/05/2022
DISTANCE	85 KM
ELEVATION	2,200 M
TOTAL TIME	12H09
MOVING TIME	11H38

SHOREHOLDER
Max Monteyne

FARO RONCADOIRA

STAGE HIGHLIGHTS

Dolos de Morás
Explore a fascinating collection of concrete structures designed to break waves.

Faro Roncadoira
This lighthouse's white silhouette contrasts beautifully against the lush hills.

Ponte da Misericordia
A stunning bridge that connects the two sides of the small town of Viveiro.

Punta Socastro
Known as "O Fuciño do Porco" or "Pig's Snout", this constructed wooden walkway weaves between the cliffs.

A Vella Ponte
A unique blend of three bridges—car, pedestrian, and train—spanning the Sor River, each adding to the scenic charm.

Estaca de Bares
The northernmost cape of the Spanish mainland.

The Loiba Coastline
Invites you to embark on a coastal walk.

STAGE STORY

One year after suffering a double leg fracture, I embarked on the seemingly mundane Stage 58, marking my first complete Galician stage. With two plates and 25 screws still in my right leg and limited training behind me, I was unsure of what this run would hold.

To manage my expectations—and perhaps avoid the embarrassment of not finishing—I chose to run anonymously. This way, I wouldn't feel the pressure of expectations, and if I fell short, I could save face. Thankfully, the stage was a bit shorter than the typical 100k, which worked in my favour.

Looking back, this low-pressure approach was likely the best mental strategy for tackling the stage. I started at an easy pace on the flat stretches, which made up most of the first half. Once the hills began, I switched to walking, knowing that speed wasn't my focus. I opted for minimal breaks, merely stopping for quick gear and food changes with Gert-Jan.

The day flew by. I felt surprisingly good, maintaining a steady, slow rhythm. To my delight, my right leg, while slightly swollen, held up well. Upon reaching the northernmost point of Spain, a rather uneventful spot, I realised I was on track to finish.

However, true to the Follow The Coast spirit, the last stretch brought its challenges. With less than 8 km to go, I faced steep climbs that turned my earlier runner's high into a mental dip.

The ascent to O Carballo and the rugged climb to O Porto de Espasante were particularly tough, requiring ropes to navigate. But the finish line was finally in sight, and I pushed through the fatigue.

A heartfelt thanks to Gert-Jan for being such a great friend and supportive crew member throughout this journey.

Stage 59

O MOSTEIRO > O BARRAL

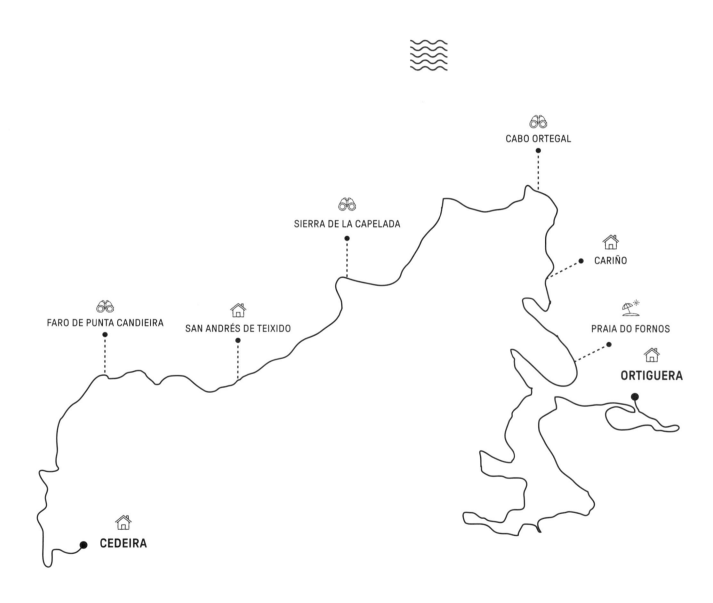

DATE	18/10/2024
DISTANCE	106.3 KM
ELEVATION	2,638 M
TOTAL TIME	14H00
MOVING TIME	13H38

SHOREHOLDER
Jonathan Fors

CABO ORTEGAL

STAGE HIGHLIGHTS

Ortigueira
Charming village on the eastern shore of the Ria de Santa Marta.

Cedeira
A picturesque town known for its sandy beaches and vibrant atmosphere.

Cariño
A delightful fishing village where you can savour the local maritime culture.

Serra da Capelada
Highest cliffs on the mainland of Europe, 621 m above sea level, offering some of the most stunning vistas imaginable. Featuring Cabo Ortegal and its iconic lighthouse, which overlooks the breathtaking cliffs of Vixía Herbeira.

San Andrés de Teixido
Isolated pilgrimage village is home to one of Galicia's most revered shrines.

Faro Punta Candieira
The scenic road adds to the allure of this lighthouse.

Praia de Fornos
Beautiful eastern-facing bay.

STAGE STORY

Oh wow, where do I even start? Meeting the crew for the first time at 5 am, clad only in their underwear, or the emotional awakening on the highest cliffs of mainland Europe? Or maybe the fact that I ran 106 km with an already injured leg? A good beginning deserves a sprinkle of context.

Ultrarunning fascinates me. While some view its participants as obsessed athletes, I see a different reality. After six years of daily running, my focus has never been on pace or competition; it's about the mental clarity it provides. Running helps me manage stress and regulate my ADHD, offering a refuge where I can think clearly.

Before diving into my experience with Stage 59 of Follow The Coast, I must share what ignited my passion for ultrarunning: a gruelling 100-mile race in northern Portugal, featuring 3,500 m of elevation gain. It was a mix of misery and beauty—34 hours of constant movement in relentless rain and 4 °C, leading to surreal hallucinations. For some, this sounds like a nightmare, but for me, it was an enlightening moment, proving that I could undertake these challenges and come out alive.

Fast forward to October 2024, and after my initial 100-mile experience just five months prior, I'd completed more 100 km runs than I could count. So when a friend invited me to join Follow The Coast for a 106 km run, I enthusiastically accepted, despite my legs still recovering from a recent 120 km race.

Now that we're all caught up, let me tell you about the run. It was beautiful.

While I could recount every lilometre, one moment stands out—around the 70 km mark, I felt a surge of enlightenment. For so long, I had pushed myself to find my limits, constantly questioning, "How far can I go?" But during this run, I realised my perspective was shifting toward simply enjoying the journey of ultrarunning.

As I ran, tears welled up as I felt an overwhelming sense of purpose and determination. I became acutely aware of how many people worldwide struggle for basic necessities, like access to clean water, while we often complain about minor inconveniences. In a world optimised for comfort, it's easy to forget our true potential.

I could go on, but I'll leave you with this: you lose what you don't use.

Stage 60

O BARRAL > FERROL

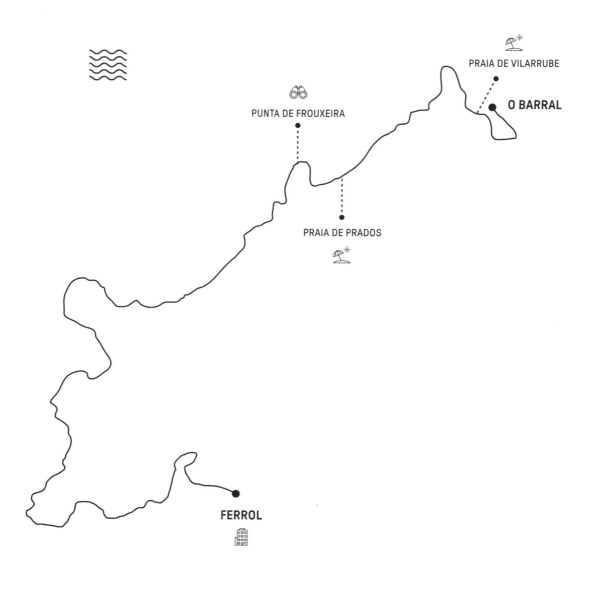

DATE	13/05/2022
DISTANCE	100 KM
ELEVATION	2,666 M
TOTAL TIME	15H25
MOVING TIME	13H44

SHOREHOLDERS
Tim Vroman
Aurillac Boury

FARO DE CABO PRIOR

STAGE HIGHLIGHTS

Ferrol
Visit the Castelo de San Felipe, a 16th-century fortress guarding the harbour, part of the "Triángulo de Fogo," which historically defended against enemy ships. Known as the birthplace of Francisco Franco, Ferrol has been a significant military base for the Spanish Northern Navy, blending natural beauty with rich historical significance.

Praia de Vilarrube
Long, serene beach nestled in Cedeira Bay.

Punta Frouxeira
Cliff with unique lighthouse set atop 20th-century concrete tunnels. Explore the nearby Praia de Prados and a charming white chapel.

Between Lavacerido and Cabo Prior
Cliffs with stunning views and small beaches formed by rivers.

The O Piero Cliffs
Your entry into the bay of Ferrol, where the iconic Hercules Tower of A Coruña can be spotted on clear days.

STAGE STORY

The alarm buzzed at 5 am, filling me with excitement as I rolled out of bed. A quick breakfast of oats fuelled my anticipation, and I began loading the "trail trunk" with gear for the day ahead. By 6.30, I was ready to wake the crew, though my first attempt was met with groggy faces and sleepy grumbles. A second attempt at 6.40 had more success, and soon we were all buzzing with energy.

At 6.55 am, it was time to go. I stood at the starting line, feeling the thrill of adventure as we set off into the dawn, the first light painting the sky in hues of orange and pink. The beauty of the coastline unfolded around us, and as we ran across hauntingly beautiful stretches of sand, pure joy surged through me.

By the time we reached the 30 km mark, reality hit. Blisters began to form, and the weight of the journey ahead pressed down on my mind. It was a moment of reckoning, a mental struggle that reminded me of the long road still to travel. But the crew rallied, and a sock change followed, accompanied by Snickers wrapped in pancakes. A quick refuel, and I was ready for the steep cliffs looming ahead.

The next stretch was a power hike through wild, overgrown paths that scraped my legs and tested my calves. Each step was a reminder of the challenges we faced. We encountered the greatest concentration of lighthouses I had ever seen, their presence both awe-inspiring and comforting. These faros became my lifeline, symbols of guidance and hope along the journey.

As the afternoon sun began to dip, we received energising support from family and friends, the Stage 61 runners cheering us on with enthusiasm that fuelled our spirits. At kilometre 70, we pushed into the unknown, both of us embarking on our longest run ever. It was a turning point; I felt Tim's struggle alongside me, a shared burden that brought us closer.

With harbour scenery in sight, we powered through, caffeine shots lighting a fire within us for the final push. Although we aimed to finish at kilometre 91, we knew there was no "Follow The Coast" stage without hitting the triple digits. So, with determination and grit, we pressed on until we finally reached kilometre 100.

As we crossed that finish line, the sun began to set, and a wave of pride washed over me. We had accomplished our mission, together as a team, and I couldn't help but think of all the faros we had encountered along the way. They had guided us home before dark, shining brightly in my memory.

Stage 61

FERROL > PUNTA TORRELLA

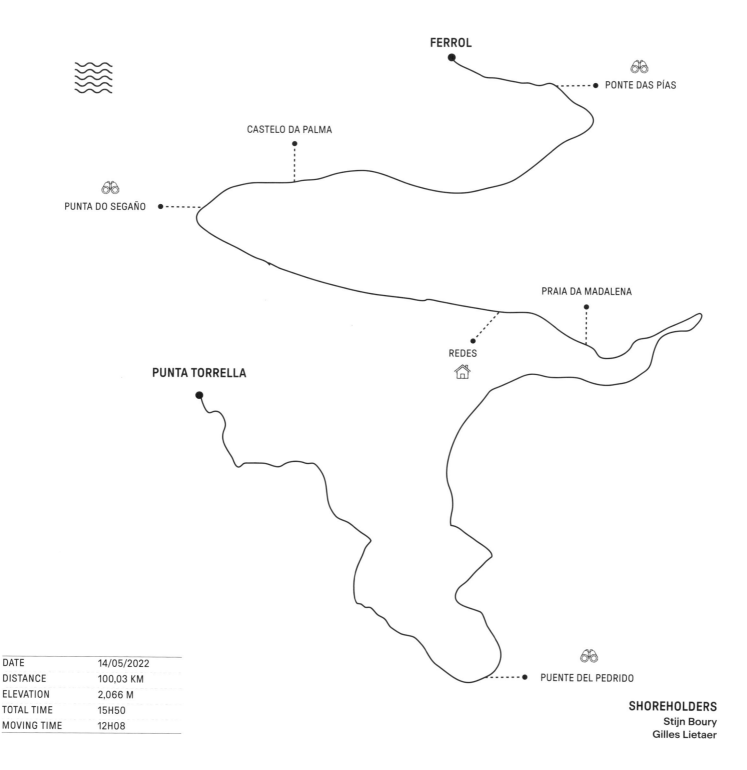

DATE	14/05/2022
DISTANCE	100,03 KM
ELEVATION	2,066 M
TOTAL TIME	15H50
MOVING TIME	12H08

SHOREHOLDERS
Stijn Boury
Gilles Lietaer

PONTE DAS PÍAS

STAGE HIGHLIGHTS

⌂ **Redes**
A picturesque fishing village in the Bay of Betanzos with vibrant houses along the water. Nearby, Praia da Madalena is a popular beach near the Río Eume, with bars, restaurants, and the Puente de Hierro train bridge creating a classic seaside view.

👀 **Ponte das Pías bridge**
Crosses Ferrol Bay, connecting the town with the historic Navantia shipyards.

👀 **Triángulo de Fogo**
Three defensive forts of Castelo da Palma, Castelo de San Felipe and San Martín on the opposite shore. Together, these forts guarded the Ferrol Bay and famously repelled the English navy in the Battle of Brión in 1800.

👀 **Punta do Segaño**
Fortified peninsula with visible remnants of underground fortifications and old artillery placements. Further west, a scenic cliff path stretches from Punta Coitelada to Arès, offering coastal views and lush landscapes.

👀 **Ponte de Pedra & Puente del Pedrido**
Two remarkable bridges respectively spanning the Río Eume and Ría Betanzos.

STAGE STORY

Longtime friends Stijn and Gilles, veterans of ultra-races and Ironmans, were ready to conquer the wild Galician coast. After a solid 82 km prep run along Belgium's coast, they knew Spain's rugged 100 km stretch would demand everything they had. The morning kicked off with early excitement after a day cheering on family through Stage 60. By 7 am, they were off... though not without a classic false start in the wrong direction! A quick pivot put them back on track across Ferrol's Ponte das Pías bridge, and soon the bustling urban scenery gave way to untouched Galician trails, where fishing villages and timeworn lighthouses appeared like celebratory checkpoints along the coast.

The first thrill came fast—a massive wild boar materialised on the trail, stopped by a fence, then hastily turned back into the forest, leaving Stijn and Gilles in stunned laughter. It was a missed photo op but an unforgettable moment. Not long after, they stumbled upon an abandoned boat, where Stijn coaxed Gilles aboard for a hilarious video–one for the day's highlight reel. Committed to completing the full 100 km, they soon found themselves hacking through trails better suited to machetes than GPS guidance. Their pace was strong, often leaving their support crew, who dashed between checkpoints by car, scrambling to keep up. By midday, the heat rose to 25 °C, and they slowed slightly to stay hydrated, fully aware that the toughest miles were yet to come.

As they climbed the cliffs near Punta Coitelada, stunning views and heart-stopping drops greeted them. A quick Coke stop in the charming village of Redes brought some energy, but cramps soon struck Stijn. Sleep-deprived and underhydrated, he had to dig deep for the remaining 45 km. Fatigue gnawed at them both, but neither would waver. Alternating between walking and running, they shared the load as a team, each stride fuelled by support and a few more sips of Coca-Cola.

The scenery only became more striking with each step, but so did the pull of exhaustion. As they neared the finish, a twist awaited: their GPS read 97 km, a cruel tease just short of the full triple digits. In one final decision, they agreed to push forward, refusing to finish shy of 100 km, crossing that mark just before nightfall. Their efforts had brought them to the coast's edge, a beer, and the immense pride of conquering one of their toughest, most scenic stages yet. It was a day marked by unexpected turns, breathtaking views, and the unbeatable grit of two determined teammates.

Stage 62

PUNTA TORRELLA > PUNTA FALSA

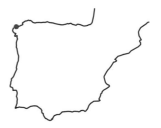

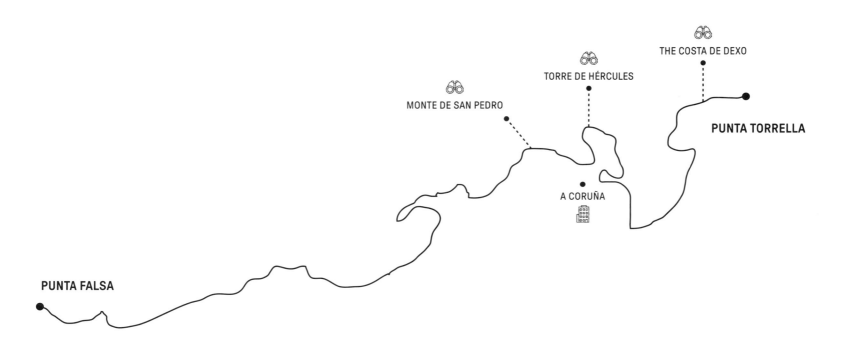

CASTELO DE SANTA CRUZ

STAGE HIGHLIGHTS

 A Coruña
Bustling port city signals a blend of maritime activity and history. The 16th-century Castelo de Santo Antón, built on a peninsula, once protected the city, while the iconic Roman Torre de Hercules — the oldest functioning lighthouse in the world — overlooks the area from a nearby hill. Close to the lighthouse lies the Campo da Rata, a poignant memorial for victims of the Franco regime. In A Coruña's historic centre, María Pita Square impresses with its grand City Hall and the hero's statue. Strolling down the Avenida de la Marina, you'll notice the classic white galleries that define the city's architecture. To cap off the journey, Monte de San Pedro provides sweeping views over the bay, city, and the Torre de Hercules.

The Costa de Dexo
A protected cape along Betanzos Bay, boasts rugged cliffs and hidden coves.

Castelo de Santa Cruz, Porto de Santa Cruz
16th-century fortress standing proudly on an island, reachable by a wooden bridge. This fortress offers a scenic detour with views over the bay.

Stage 63

PUNTA FALSA > AROU

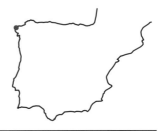

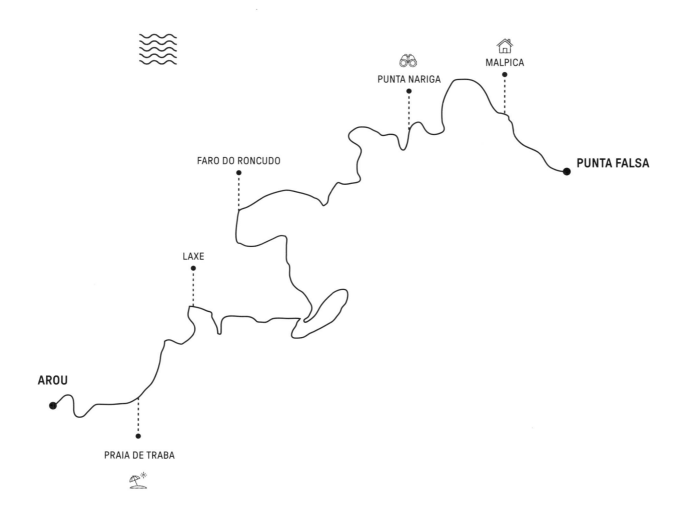

DATE	30/04/2023
DISTANCE	90.5 KM
ELEVATION	2,713 M
TOTAL TIME	14H36
MOVING TIME	14H09

SHOREHOLDER
Max Monteyne

DUNAS DE TRABA

STAGE HIGHLIGHTS

A beautiful remote, rugged stretch of Galicia with winding trails run along steep, lush cliffs and down into small, hidden bays with clear blue waters and pristine, white-sand beaches.

Malpica
The fishing village marking the start of the Costa da Morte, a famed and treacherous shoreline where shipwrecks dot the rocks along this legendary "Coast of Death".

Punta Nariga
From Praia Barizo to Faro do Roncudo, the GR trail twists along Punta Nariga, a demanding route known for its rough terrain.

Monte Branco
Offers panoramic views of the Punta de Balares sandbank, an impressive formation created by the Río Anllóns.

Praia de Traba
Vast white beach, bordered by bird-breeding dunes.

STAGE STORY

Finally picking up after some challenging COVID years, I had the chance to run the first stage of 2023. For the first time, I had the company and support of my parents, who were on vacation in Spain and Portugal, and my dog Julien, who decided to play a big role toward the end of the stage!

I'll never forget what popped up on my watch after just 10 m of running: "hill 1/45." Mapping the stage, I knew it would be hilly, but seeing that message made it crystal clear: this was not going to be a fast stage. I started on a beach and was immediately greeted by a steep hill that marked the first 2.5 km. If I wanted to survive this stage, I had to take it slow. And slow it was.

The first 15 km felt fantastic, but the terrain quickly became much more challenging. Steep hills, tiny trails, bushes, and rocks made each step a struggle, and the pace was agonisingly slow. After 5 hours, I had barely covered 30 km. I kept calculating how much longer it would take, but the views kept me going.

I had to make peace with my slow pace, but the real challenge came when I couldn't find my crew. I desperately needed food and water, but then, through the mist, the Faro de came into view. Seeing my support crew again filled me with energy. With fresh supplies, I was ready to tackle the next 40 km of winding single trails, which were often hard to find. Despite the frustration, the beauty of the landscape kept me motivated.

After 65 km, I got another supply, and finally, I was able to run some stretches, thanks to longer, flatter sections. My legs felt surprisingly good, but at kilometre 80, exhaustion hit hard. The climb up the final hills was brutal, but I kept counting down the "last 10 hills," hoping for the end. When I passed a sign reading "Costa da Morte," it perfectly summed up how I felt.

With less than 15 km to go, I decided to run with Julien for motivation. Everything was going well until he ran off, and I lost him in a rocky stretch. Panic set in as I spent 45 minutes screaming his name, running up and down, when Gert-Jan came back from the finish line, and my parents searched the last village. Just as I was losing hope, a notification from Julien's Airtag arrived—he had been found! It was a relief to know he was safe, and I could finally finish the stage. This challenging yet beautiful day made me fall in love with Galicia.

Stage 64

AROU > FRIXE

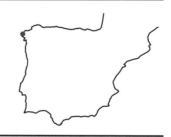

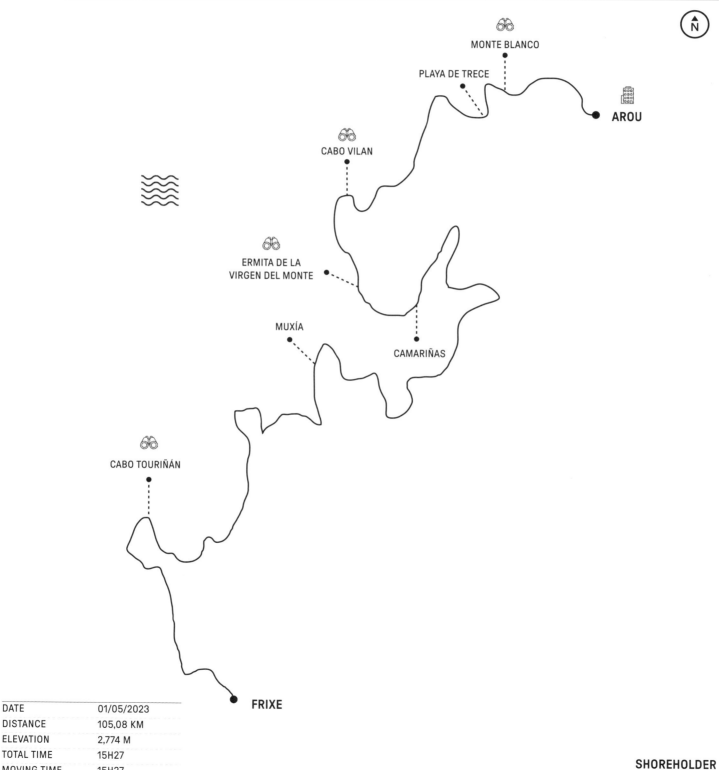

DATE	01/05/2023
DISTANCE	105,08 KM
ELEVATION	2,774 M
TOTAL TIME	15H27
MOVING TIME	15H27

SHOREHOLDER
Hung Nguyen

MIRADOIRO DA FURNA DO SAPO

STAGE HIGHLIGHTS

Arou
This charming Galician fishing village, is known for its colourful houses that line the waterfront, creating a picturesque scene.

Monte Blanco
A hill partly covered in white sand, blown from the nearby Playa de Trece.

Punta Cabo Vilan
Twin lighthouses standing tall against the backdrop of the Atlantic Ocean.

Ermita de la Virgen del Monte
Pilgrimage overlooking a hill on the Costa da Morte, offering views from the Camariñas Bay toward Muxía, home to the Santuario de la Virgen de la Barca, whose rock formations are magnificent.

Cabo Touriñán
Marks the most western point of the Spanish mainland, a small peninsula north of Cabo Fisterra.

Lires Camino
A section of the famous GR trail, that provides a lovely, peaceful walk through scenic countryside and coastal paths.

STAGE STORY

My name is Hung Nguyen, and I'm 41 years old, hailing from the Netherlands. Although my passion for running is a relatively recent discovery, sports have always been a fundamental part of my life. As a child, I started with kung fu and soccer, which laid the foundation for my love of movement and discipline. At 19, I ventured into weightlifting, and that moment changed my life. Over the next two decades, fitness became a core element of who I am—always pushing myself to grow stronger, both physically and mentally. I found strength in challenges, and fitness became my personal journey of self-discovery.

It wasn't until 2019 that I truly discovered running. My older sister, a marathon runner, was the one who inspired me to sign up for my first half marathon in Amsterdam. The experience was nothing short of transformative. After crossing that finish line, I was hooked. Running provided something unique—a way to push my limits, not just physically but mentally, and it gave me the freedom to connect with nature in a way I had never experienced before. The feeling of completing a race was unlike any other, and it sparked a deeper desire to explore the world of running.

After a few half marathons, I set my sights on my first full marathon in 2020. That challenge opened up a whole new world for me, and I quickly realised that my true passion lay in long-distance trail running, especially ultramarathons. The thrill of navigating challenging trails, covering long distances, and pushing my body to its limits became addictive. When I first heard about Follow The Coast, I was immediately intrigued by the idea of running such an incredible and scenic route. Without hesitation, I signed up for Stage 64, excited for the new adventure ahead.

Running through nature has become a form of self-expression for me. It's a journey of both physical and mental exploration, one where I find strength, peace, and resilience. Each run offers a new perspective, and every race is an opportunity to push my boundaries.
For me, running is not just about the finish line; it's about the process, the growth, and the connection to the world around me. Through my experiences, I hope to inspire others to embrace their own challenges, tap into their inner strength, and fully engage with the beauty and energy that life has to offer. Whether it's in nature or in life, every step counts.

Stage 65

FRIXE > PUNTA CANTÓN

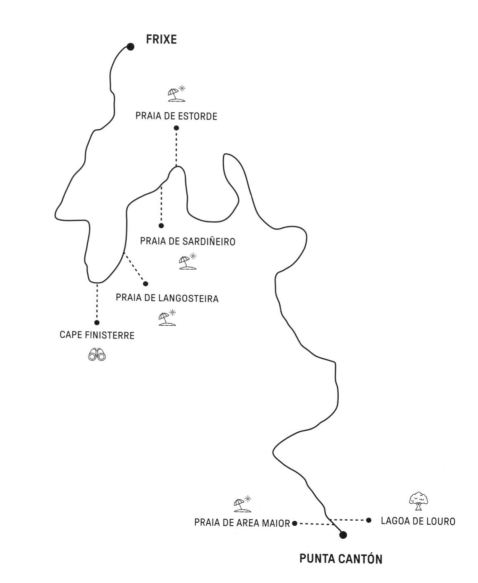

DATE	02/05/2023
DISTANCE	76,2 KM
ELEVATION	1,783 M
TOTAL TIME	16H50
MOVING TIME	11H52

SHOREHOLDERS
Ann Vanden Wyngaerd
Ilse Vleminck

FARO DE CABO CEE

FARO DE FISTERRA

STAGE HIGHLIGHTS

 Cabo Finistere
Cabo Finistere, a lighthouse perched on rocky cliffs, marking the "end of the known world".

 Praia de Estorde
Features calm, crystalline waters, perfect for a refreshing swim.

 Praia de Langosteira
A long beach with clear waters and golden sands, offering views back toward Finisterre, popular with pilgrims concluding the Camino de Santiago.

 Praia de Sardiñeiro
A picturesque beach backed by lush green hills and fishing villages, offering an authentic glimpse into Galician coastal life.

 Lagoa de Louro
A freshwater lagoon adjacent to Praia de Area Maior, providing a peaceful haven for birdlife and a contrast to Galicia's rugged cliffs.

 Praia de Area Maior
Located near Louro, this beach boasts brilliant blue waters with Monte Louro rising in the background, offering a scenic coastal experience.

STAGE STORY

Stage 65 was Ilse's second and my third. Our adventure took an unexpected twist when our original Ryanair flight was cancelled, forcing us to tackle this stage on a different date and without any support crew. It became an adventure within the adventure—braving brutal, unspoiled nature where the trails were so overgrown they were barely accessible. Of all the stages, this one was by far the most unique, offering breathtaking views and dramatic landscapes that were both humbling and awe-inspiring.

We spent hours running, getting stuck, retracing our steps, falling, and picking ourselves up again. We were forced off the route several times, heading toward small signs of civilisation to knock on doors and ask for water and an apple from one of the many locals named Maria. The magic of Finisterra, the so-called "end of the world," added to the surreal feeling of the day. By the time we'd covered 25 km, we'd already been on the move for over seven hours, climbed more than 1,000 m, and were starting to feel the weight of the day. A creeping sense of doubt lingered—would we make it to the end?

At one point, with 37 km still to go, I wrote the following words: "Many ups and downs. Sometimes you're on a path, thinking everything's going well, and then suddenly the path disappears. You fall, you stand back up. Sometimes it hurts. Sometimes you think you won't make it. But then you straighten up and move forward, step by step. And somehow, you get there. There are people who care about you, who cheer you on, and in those tough moments, it moves you, and you might shed a tear. Trail running is like life, living fully."

These words kept us going, reminding us of the resilience we both carry. Each step forward felt like a victory, every fall a chance to rise stronger. In the end, it was the love for the journey, the connection with each other, and the encouragement of those who support us that carried us through. Trail running, like life itself, is about embracing every high and low, each moment of despair and triumph, with an open heart.

Stage 66

PUNTA CANTÓN > CORRUBEDO

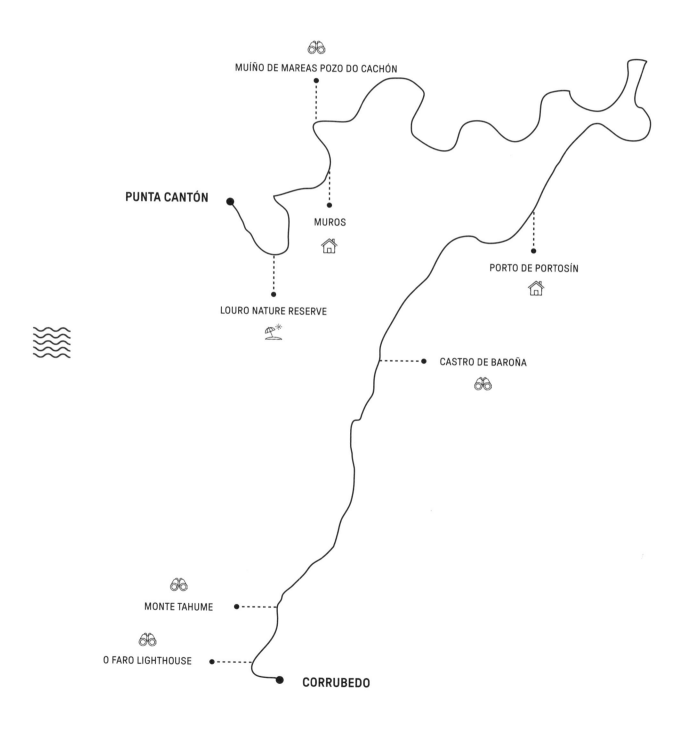

PRAIA DE LARIÑO

FARO DE MONTE LOURO

STAGE HIGHLIGHTS

⌂ **Muros**
A charming fishing village surrounded by the scenic Ría de Muros y Noia, the first of four deep bays along Galicia's southern coast.

 Muíño de Mareas Pozo do Cachón
An ancient tidal mill, keypart of the region's history.

 Ponte Testal
A modest, quiet harbour with colourful fishing boats.

⌂ **Porto de Portosín**
This harbour town offers a quieter stop.

 Castro de Baroña
An ancient Celtic fortification with panoramic views.

⛱ **Louro Nature Reserve**
A wide, west-facing beach in front of a lagoon, with a hill rising 40 m.

 Monte Tahume
A climb to this peak rewards visitors with great vantage points over the bay.

 O Faro Lighthouse
Iconic lighthouse, accessed via a dramatic, straight road perfect for pictures.

Stage 67

CORRUBEDO > CATOIRA

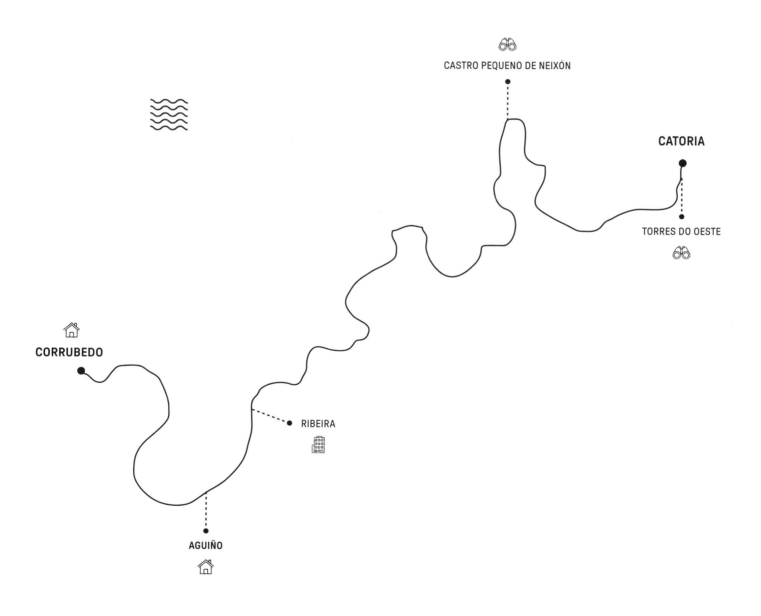

DATE	04/05/2023
DISTANCE	96 KM
ELEVATION	1,400 M
TOTAL TIME	14H20
MOVING TIME	12H44

SHOREHOLDER
Anna Simonsson-Søndenå

PRAIA DA LADEIRA

STAGE HIGHLIGHTS

 Corrubedo
A charming fishing village, with the house of architect David Chipperfield, surrounded by the Dunes of Corrubedo and the Laguna de Carregal.

 Aguiño
A small fishing village where the Ponte do Carreiro spans the river.

Ribeira
The capital of the Barbanza comarca, a bustling port town contrasting with the nature around.

 Ría de Arousa
The northern part of the second-largest bay in southern Galicia, offering stunning coastal views.

 Castro Pequeno de Neixón
An ancient Celtic settlement on a small peninsula.

 Torre do Oeste
Ninth-century towers built by the Spanish king to defend against Viking raids.

 Catoira
A site where Viking influence remains, featuring remnants of Viking boats and statues commemorating their 8th-century presence.

STAGE STORY

Is this really what I should be doing at 20? Aren't I supposed to be studying or getting a "real" job to prepare for life? These were the questions that crossed my mind as my feet burned from the pressure of the 79 km I had already covered. So, what's this all about? Why am I doing this? Or rather, why are we doing this? Hundreds of us are on this journey together.

My story began 11 days earlier. I had just completed a 165 km run through the Lofoten Islands in Norway, the furthest I'd ever run, and I did it with a smile. I've run many ultras before, but the 165 km felt controlled, despite the challenges. But running 165 km just days before a 100 km stage in Galicia? That's a recipe for failure, right? Yet, I knew if I was strong enough, I'd push through.

Travelling to Spain after a feverish night, I arrived at a welcoming house and prepared for the run. Despite the exhaustion, the excitement built as the full moon lit up the sky. I didn't know much about the course, and that's part of the thrill—the adventure of not knowing.

The first 25 km went smoothly. I love the pain of hard work, the anticipation of the unknown. But after 30 km, I felt a familiar discomfort. I adjusted my carb intake, listened to my body, and powered through. By 53 km, I gained a second wind running through a village that looked like it was made of Legos, bright and inviting.

At 65 km, tired legs needed fuel. A Snickers pancake and some caffeine helped, but I was struggling. Then, I FaceTimed a follower for some encouragement, and we became good friends. The pain hit harder as the run wore on. At 79 km, my feet burned, and that's when willpower kicked in. The last stretch was a mental battle, but I found that extra gear—the one that taps into your deepest reserves.

As I neared the finish, I smiled running up the last hill with "From Now On" blaring from the car speakers. Finally, I reached the Viking ship at the end of the run, and everything felt perfect. Being from Scandinavia, it was a fitting end to the day.

So, why did I do this? I realised there's a spark inside me that shines brightest when I push myself like this. It brings me joy in its purest form. This is what I want to do—run and share my journey. It's my dream life, and I'm living it. My message: Follow your dreams and do what makes you happy. The pieces of your perfect puzzle will fall into place, and you'll have a life full of joy and colour.

Stage 68

CATOIRA > ILLA DA TOXA

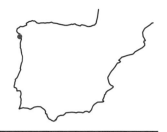

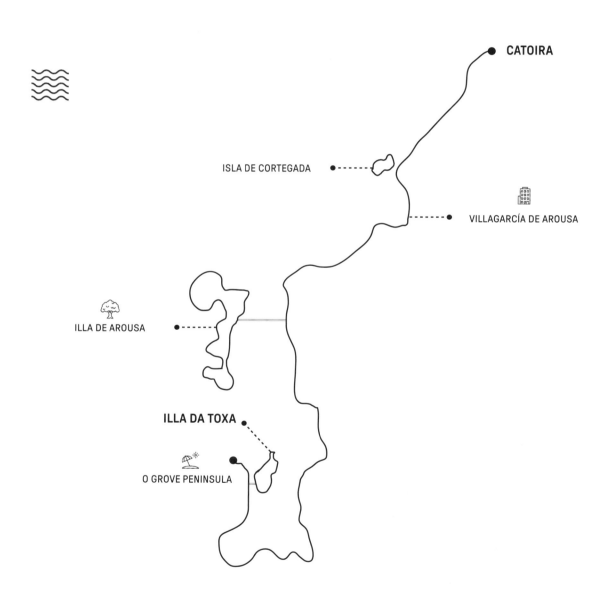

- CATOIRA
- ISLA DE CORTEGADA
- VILLAGARCÍA DE AROUSA
- ILLA DE AROUSA
- ILLA DA TOXA
- O GROVE PENINSULA

SHOREHOLDER
Federica Panzarella

ILLA DE AROUSA

STAGE HIGHLIGHTS

 Villagarcía de Arousa
A charming coastal town featuring beaches like Compostela Beach and access to Cortegada Island, a protected natural area.

 Ría de Arousa
A stunning estuary along the southern edge, known for its pristine natural beauty and scenic islands like Isla de Arosa and Isla de Cortegada.

 Ponte da Illa de Arousa
An impressive 2 km bridge connecting the mainland to Isla de Arousa, offering access to beaches like Playa de Area da Secada and Playa de Bao.

 Faro de Punta Cabalo
A lighthouse built in 1852 on the northern tip of Illa de Arousa, with breathtaking views over the bay.

 O Grove Peninsula
Known for its scenic, turquoise water beaches and world-renowned seafood.

 Illa da Toxa
A tranquil island famous for its luxury spas, providing a peaceful retreat.

STAGE STORY

The 100 km solo run along the Galician coast from Catoira to Illa da Toxa began under a gentle drizzle. The cool rain felt refreshing, almost like a cleansing ritual, marking the start of a journey that would take me deep into my thoughts. At first, I focused on the mechanics of running—the rhythm of my breath, the pounding of my heart, and the careful placement of my feet. But as the kilometres ticked by, the world around me faded, and I found myself immersed in reflection. The solitude of the run allowed my mind to wander freely, and I thought about what drove me to seek discomfort and push my limits. Each step became a conversation with myself, a dialogue of self-discovery.

As the rain eased and the sun broke through, the landscape transformed. The warmth of the sun energised me, bringing a renewed sense of clarity. Each stride in the sunlight felt invigorating, providing a welcome shift in my pace. Running through the small villages along the way, I was struck by the simple joys of human connection. Locals greeted me with smiles, and I exchanged a few encouraging words with fellow runners I encountered. These brief interactions reminded me of the importance of community, even in moments of solitude. It was as if the universe was reinforcing that, while I was undertaking this challenge alone, I was never truly solitary; I was part of a larger tapestry of human experience.

As I neared Illa da Toxa, the sunset painted the sky in vibrant colours, creating a beautiful backdrop for reflection. I was filled with gratitude—not just for the scenery, but for the lessons learned along the way. The physical struggle had mirrored the emotional journey, each step reminding me of my resilience and capacity for growth. It became clear that this run was about more than just distance; it was a path to understanding myself better.

Crossing the finish line brought a sense of triumph. Yet, the days that followed were filled with blisters, resulting in a penguin-like gait! Each painful step served as a humorous reminder of the challenge I embraced. Ultimately, it was a small price to pay for an unforgettable experience that would resonate long after the blisters healed.

Stage 69

ILLA DA TOXA > CABO UDRA

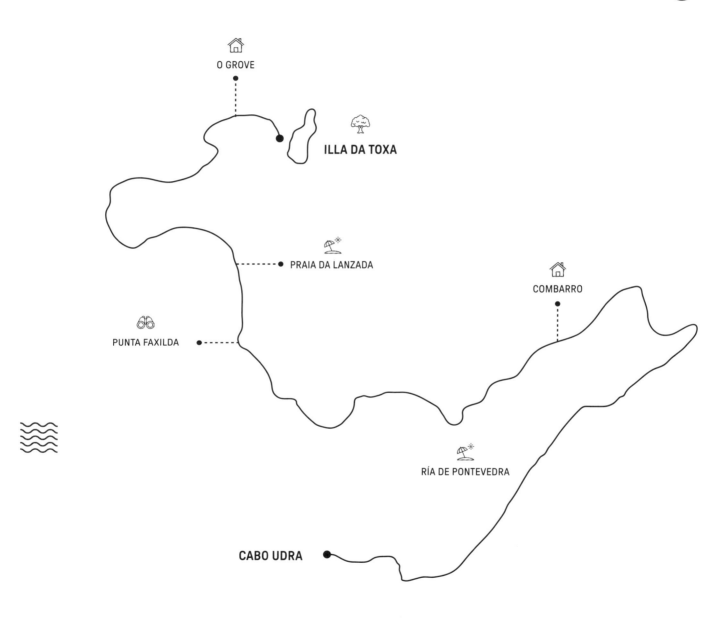

RÍAS BAIXAS, COMBARRO

STAGE HIGHLIGHTS

 Illa da Toxa
Famed for its thermal spas and the scallop-covered Capilla de las Conchas.

 O Grove
A charming fishing village celebrated for its world-class seafood and sandy beaches like Praia de Mexilloeira, blending gastronomy and relaxation.

 Sanxenxo
Galicia's bustling beach capital, with lively promenades and golden sands.

 Combarro
A picturesque village known for its stone granaries and cobblestone streets.

 Praia da Lanzada
A 2.5 km stretch of pristine sand, ideal for surfers.

 Punta Faxilda
Dramatic cliffs complemented by the tranquil coves at Punta Cabicastro.

 Ría de Pontevedra
A coastline dotted with fishing villages and white-sand beaches.

Stage 70

CABO UDRA > PRAIA DE PATOS

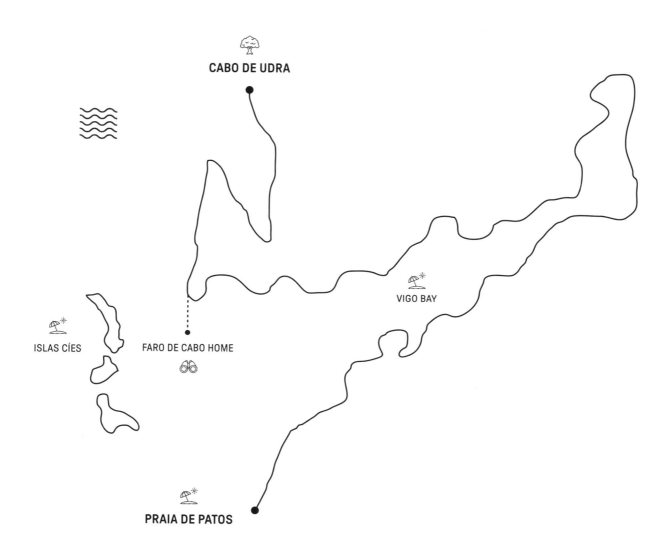

DATE	07/05/2023
DISTANCE	108,17 KM
ELEVATION	1,788 M
TOTAL TIME	14H42
MOVING TIME	13H29

SHOREHOLDERS
Xander De Buysscher
Senne Vandevenne

PRAIA DE VILARIÑO

FARO DE CABO HOME

STAGE HIGHLIGHTS

Cabo Udra
A dramatic start with rugged cliffs and pristine beauty, offering sweeping views of the Atlantic and the entrance to the Ría de Pontevedra.

Islas Cíes
Three stunning islands, part of the Parque Nacional Marítimo-Terrestre das Illas Atlánticas, renowned for their unspoiled beaches and clear waters, often likened to the Caribbean.

Faro de Cabo Home
An iconic lighthouse near Donón, perched on a windswept promontory, providing breathtaking views of the Atlantic Ocean and the Islas Cíes.

Vigo Bay
A blend of rocky shores and sandy beaches, transitioning the coastline into a vibrant mix of natural and urban beauty.

Praia de Patos
A lively beach popular among surfers for its consistent waves.

STAGE STORY

It had been a dream of mine for a couple of years to run a stage of Follow The Coast. Finally, I took the leap and asked my friend Xander if he wanted to join me. He said yes without hesitation, even though we had never run together before. We chose this stage in Galicia, not overthinking what kind of landscapes or terrain awaited us. This would be the first 100 km run for both of us—a challenge we were eager to embrace.

The day started under a thick, early-morning fog that soon gave way to a warm sun and a light, refreshing breeze. What unfolded was a stunning journey across an incredible variety of terrains: long, golden beaches, rocky ascents, rainforest-like woods, stretches along railroad tracks, bustling harbour quays, and even the busy streets of Vigo. Each segment brought new surprises. We passed majestic lighthouses, massive bridges, and fascinating buildings, all blending into the unique character of Galicia's coastline. Yet, much of the run was spent in serene, untouched nature, where the only sounds were our footsteps and the whisper of the wind.

The energy from the crew kept us going. Every time we reached their checkpoint, they greeted us with food, drinks, and words of encouragement that filled us with perseverance. Their enthusiasm was infectious and carried us forward through the tough stretches.

As we approached the finish line, near the point where the crew and the next stage runner waited, a wave of emotion surged through us. The sense of accomplishment and the shared effort made the moment unforgettable. I'll never forget the heroic chill that coursed through my body as we passed them.

This 108 km stage wasn't just a milestone in distance—it was the first time Xander and I ran together. What began as a shared challenge turned into the foundation of a beautiful friendship. The day was perfect in so many ways, and the experience was one we'll carry with us forever. It won't be our last stage—this is only the beginning.

Stage 71

PRAIA DE PATOS > FONTELA

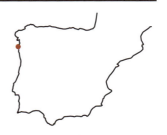

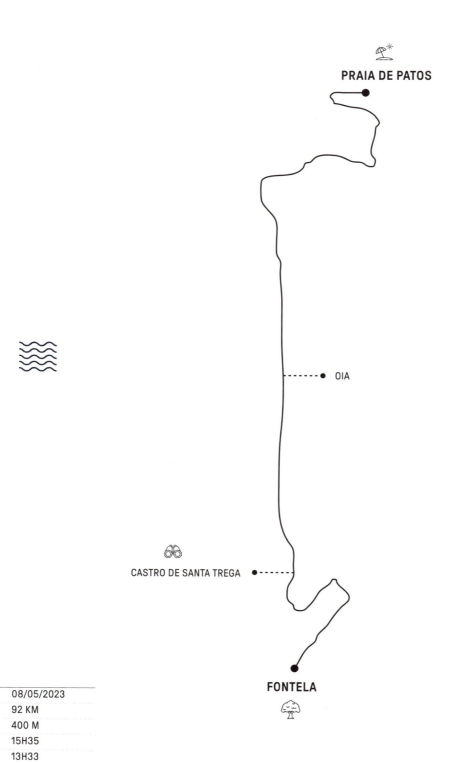

DATE	08/05/2023
DISTANCE	92 KM
ELEVATION	400 M
TOTAL TIME	15H35
MOVING TIME	13H33

SHOREHOLDER
Federico Fiz

FARO DE CABO SILLEIRO

STAGE HIGHLIGHTS

 Praia de Patos
A golden-sand beach in Nigrán, offering the tranquil sound of waves and a refreshing sea breeze, perfect for a peaceful start to the journey.

 Castro de Santa Tegra
An ancient Celtic settlement on a hilltop near A Guarda, providing panoramic views of the River Miño's mouth and the Atlantic Ocean, as well as fascinating Iron Age archaeological remains.

 Fontela
A remote coastal area near Oia, known for its dramatic cliffs, unspoiled beauty, and the soothing sound of waves crashing against the rocks.

STAGE STORY

Having survived Stage 54 alongside my wife (and somehow managing not to blame her entirely for our lack of preparation), I approached my second stage, Stage 71, with the misguided optimism that a bit of training would make everything easier. Spoiler alert: it didn't. Unlike the improvised chaos of the first stage, this one was supposed to have structure—or at least my version of it. Think haphazard training paired with a mental spreadsheet full of "ifs" and "maybes." This time, there was no Stéphanie to blame and no ensaimadas to boost morale. Just me, the rugged Galician coast, and the delusion that my body was still ten years younger. The stage started deceptively well: sunny skies, 100% motivation, and the promise of a scenic day in nature. That optimism lasted about three kilometres, right until I hit my first climb—a steep one designed to reward you with breathtaking views. And by you, I mean you, because I barely had the energy to notice them. With that box checked, I pushed on to Bayona, a charming town where I fuelled up with a bullet coffee. Magic potion, they say. Spoiler alert #2: it's not magic.

Being a methodical sort, I'd divided the stage into four blocks. The first block ended with a mix of pedestrians and bustling towns—manageable. The second, a marathon-length straight road, seemed perfect for settling into a steady pace. But here's the thing about straight roads: they fool you into running faster than you should, and you end up paying the price. And oh, did I pay. That thin line between believing you can run two marathons in a row and realising you can't? I crossed it. Follow the Coast doesn't need steep climbs or treacherous descents to humble you. Sometimes, it's just your own overconfidence that sends you soaring, only to drop you into the mud. The final two blocks were a mental marathon. At one point, I could see the finish line—except to reach it, I had to cross a bridge 25 km inland. Multiply that by two, and suddenly, going back home to Mallorca sounded like the better plan.

Thankfully, I wasn't alone. Stéphanie kept me going through the first half, and Max took over for the second. Conversations, humility, and a cocktail of caffeine pills and Red Bulls pushed me through the cold, rainy night to the finish line in the beautiful town of Moledo.

Why do I put myself through this? To prepare for when quitting isn't an option. If the lone wolf dies, I'm grateful this wolf had the stubbornness of the pack to keep moving forward.

↪ Regions 5 / 10
Norte

21,278 km²
3.6 million inhabitants

→ ESPOSENDE

PRAIA DO CAMARIDO, CAMINHA

↳ The northernmost region of Portugal, Norte is a land of rich contrasts where rolling green hills and rugged mountains blend seamlessly with historic towns and a dramatic coastline. Known as the birthplace of the nation, this region is steeped in cultural and natural beauty, offering visitors a glimpse into Portugal's soul.

With its temperate Atlantic climate, Norte boasts lush vineyards that produce the famous Vinho Verde, verdant forests and fertile valleys carved by the Douro River. Its coastline features sweeping beaches and picturesque fishing villages, while inland, the landscape transforms into terraced slopes and granite peaks.

Home to a rich diversity of flora and fauna, the region is a haven for nature lovers, offering idyllic settings for hiking, birdwatching, or simply immersing oneself in its serene beauty. From the historic city of Porto to the tranquil Peneda-Gerês National Park, Norte captures the essence of Portugal's heritage and natural splendour.

Norte

113 km Coastline
Capital: Porto

Norte
↳ Introduction

HOW TO GET AROUND

If you want to visit the Norte region, Porto is your central hub. Caminha, the northern town at the Spanish border, is a 1-hour drive away, similar to the 45 minutes you'll spend driving to Aveiro.

Porto has an international airport, or you can find alternatives in Lisbon, but you'll need to account for a 3-hour drive to reach Porto. If you enjoy wine, the Douro vineyards farther inland make for an interesting destination.

WHERE TO STAY

For a coastal getaway in Portugal's Norte region, you'll find a diverse range of accommodations blending comfort, charm and local culture.

In Vila do Conde, boutique guesthouses provide a mix of history and proximity to golden beaches, making it a great spot for relaxation. Nearby, Póvoa de Varzim features modern hotels with ocean views, perfect for unwinding after exploring its vibrant promenade and traditional markets.

In Porto, elegant seaside hotels in the Foz do Douro district offer luxury, serene sunsets, and easy access to the city's lively atmosphere, port wine cellars, and iconic landmarks.

Further along the coast, smaller fishing villages like Esposende offer cozy inns that reflect the maritime heritage of the region, ideal for immersing yourself in local traditions. From Porto's dynamic energy to the tranquil charm of the Norte's coastline, you'll find accommodations that cater to every taste and experience.

HISTORY

The coastal part of Portugal's Norte region has a rich and layered history shaped by its relationship with the Atlantic Ocean. This area was a key hub during the Roman era, evident in ancient salt production sites like those near Esposende.

During the Age of Discoveries, ports like Porto and Vila do Conde became pivotal for maritime trade, building the ships that carried explorers to new worlds. Fishing villages like Póvoa de Varzim flourished as centres of maritime activity, renowned for their skilled fishermen and vibrant traditions.

The region also saw Viking incursions, leaving traces in local folklore and defensive structures. In the medieval period, the Norte's coastal towns thrived through commerce thanks to their strategic location. Today, traditions such as bobbin lace-making and festivals rooted in seafaring heritage reflect the enduring connection between the Norte's people and the sea, making its coastline a living museum of Portugal's maritime past.

NORTE

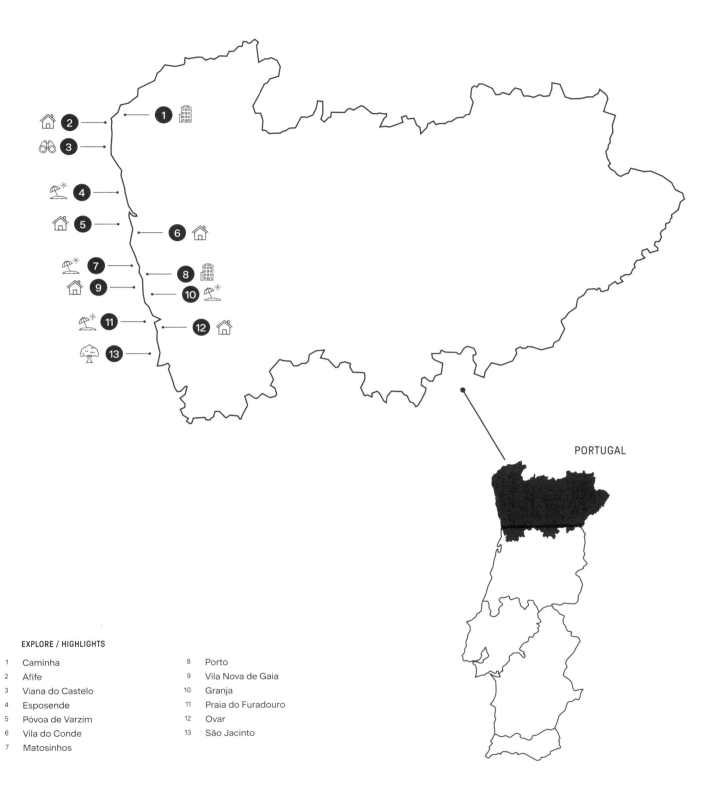

EXPLORE / HIGHLIGHTS

1. Caminha
2. Afife
3. Viana do Castelo
4. Esposende
5. Póvoa de Varzim
6. Vila do Conde
7. Matosinhos
8. Porto
9. Vila Nova de Gaia
10. Granja
11. Praia do Furadouro
12. Ovar
13. São Jacinto

REGION 5 / 10

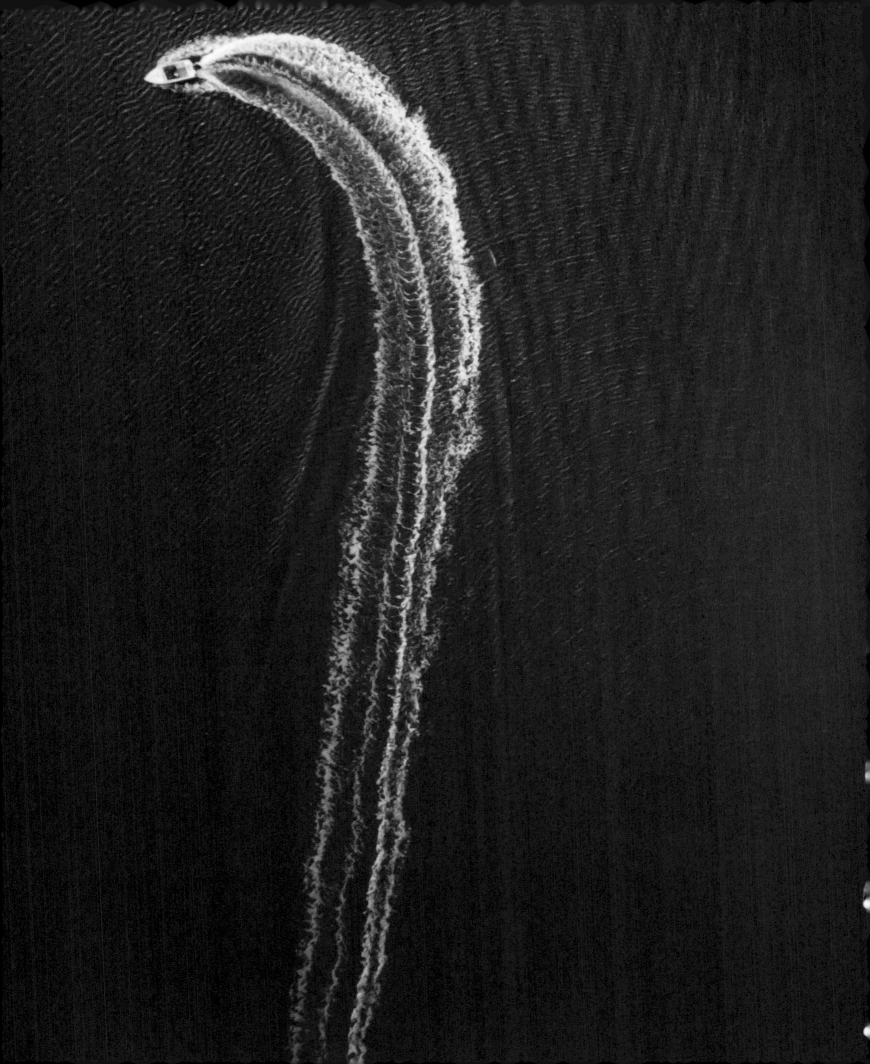

Norte
↳ Highlights

The coastal stretch of Portugal's Norte region, anchored by the vibrant city of Porto, offers a stunning blend of rugged beauty, cultural charm and urban sophistication. Porto enchants with its UNESCO-listed Ribeira district, colourful riverside houses, and iconic Dom Luís I Bridge. Along the coast, golden beaches like Espinho and Foz do Douro attract surfers and sunseekers, while chic promenades and scenic sunsets offer urban elegance.

Beyond Porto, fishing towns like Vila do Conde and Póvoa de Varzim exude maritime heritage, where fishing boats line the harbours and the aroma of grilled sardines fills the air. Explore vibrant markets, watch artisans craft rendas de bilros lace, or savour arroz de marisco by the sea. From Porto's historic port wine cellars to the wild Atlantic swells, the Norte coast is a celebration of natural beauty and authentic Portuguese culture.

1. CAMINHA

At the mouth of the Minho River, Caminha offers a picturesque blend of river and sea. Visit the Matriz Church, explore the medieval walls, and relax at Moledo Beach, a serene spot with views of the Santa Tecla Mountain in Spain.

2. AFIFE

A tranquil village near Viana do Castelo, Afife boasts white sand beaches, a vast dune system and strong waves ideal for surfers. The surrounding Santa Luzia mountains offer hiking trails with stunning views of the Atlantic Ocean.

3. VIANA DO CASTELO

A coastal gem, Viana do Castelo is known for the hilltop Santa Luzia Basilica, offering panoramic ocean views. The town's old quarter features traditional architecture and museums. Nearby Cabedelo Beach is a hotspot for windsurfing and kitesurfing.

4. ESPOSENDE

Located on the Cávado River estuary, this charming coastal town is surrounded by sandy beaches. Explore Ofir Beach, a popular spot for surfing, and enjoy hiking in the Northern Litoral Natural Park, known for its dunes, birdlife and stunning ocean views.

Esposende is also part of the Camino Portuguese Coastal Route, a scenic path for pilgrims heading to Santiago de Compostela, offering serene landscapes and historical landmarks. Don't miss the row of ancient windmills (now used as summer houses) that line Apúlia Beach, to the south of the town.

5. PÓVOA DE VARZIM

A lively beach town with a long history, Póvoa de Varzim features sandy shores, a bustling casino, and a vibrant promenade. The Fort of Nossa Senhora da Conceição adds historical charm to this seaside destination.

6. VILA DO CONDE

A picturesque coastal town with sandy beaches and rich history. Visit the imposing Monastery of Santa Clara, explore the traditional shipyard museum, and relax along the scenic coastline, where fishing traditions meet modern leisure.

7. MATOSINHOS

Located just outside Porto, Matosinhos is a culinary and beach haven. Known for its seafood restaurants and urban charm, it offers a wide beach perfect for surfing. Visit the striking Tidal Pools of Leça, designed in the 1960s by the great Portuguese architect Álvaro Siza Vieira.

8. PORTO

This vibrant coastal city enchants with its historic Ribeira district, a UNESCO World Heritage site brimming with colourful houses and cobblestone streets. Stroll along the Douro River, lined with lively cafes and traditional rabelo boats, and cross the iconic Dom Luís I Bridge for panoramic views. Don't miss the stunning Livraria Lello,

PRAIA DO SENHOR DA PEDRA

ESPOSENDE NATURAL PARK

one of the world's most beautiful bookstores, or the majestic Clérigos Tower for sweeping city vistas.

The São Bento Railway Station dazzles with its blue-and-white azulejo tiles depicting Portuguese history. Nearby, Foz do Douro offers golden beaches, scenic promenades, and a perfect blend of urban charm and coastal serenity. Indulge in local delicacies like francesinha sandwiches and pastel de nata, while soaking in Porto's unique atmosphere.

9. VILA NOVA DE GAIA

Across the Douro from Porto, Vila Nova de Gaia is famed for its port wine cellars and stunning views of Porto's skyline. Walk along the riverfront, enjoy wine tastings, or visit the sandy beaches of Praia de Lavadores. The area's cable car offers sweeping coastal and city vistas.

10. GRANJA

One of Portugal's oldest and most charming seaside resorts, Granja Beach near Espinho, just to the south of Porto, features 19th-century architecture, reflecting its history as a retreat for Portuguese elites.

The beach is calm, making it suitable for families. Walk along the wooden boardwalk, admire elegant villas, or relax in its laid-back ambiance. Granja is a delightful mix of historical charm and coastal serenity.

11. PRAIA DO FURADOURO

This stunning Atlantic coastline spot near Ovar is ideal for a relaxing day out. Known for its scenic views, it's popular with windsurfers and kite surfers due to favourable winds. The beach is lined with seafood restaurants offering fresh catches, such as grilled fish and octopus. The promenade is perfect for a leisurely walk or to catch the sunset. It's a great place for unwinding in nature.

12. OVAR

Ovar is a picturesque town known for its azulejo, the traditional Portuguese tiles that adorn its architecture. Wander the streets to admire these colourful façades or visit the Igreja Matriz for its stunning tilework.

The town is also famous for its vibrant carnival, one of Portugal's largest, and you can learn all about this festive tradition at the city's museum. Ovar's culinary highlight is pão-de-ló, a rich sponge cake that pairs wonderfully with coffee.

13. SÃO JACINTO

This natural reserve offers tranquil landscapes of sand dunes, pine forests and wetlands. It's a haven for birdwatchers and hikers, with trails that wind through this protected area. Rare bird species, including flamingos, can be spotted.

A ferry from Aveiro provides access to this serene escape. São Jacinto is perfect for reconnecting with nature and enjoying Portugal's unspoiled beauty.

DOM LUIS I BRIDGE, PORTO   DOURO, PORTO

↰ FURADOURO　　　　　　　　　　　　　　　　　　　　　　　　　　　　PONTE DA BARRINHA ↗

Stage 72

FONTELA > MINDELO

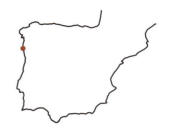

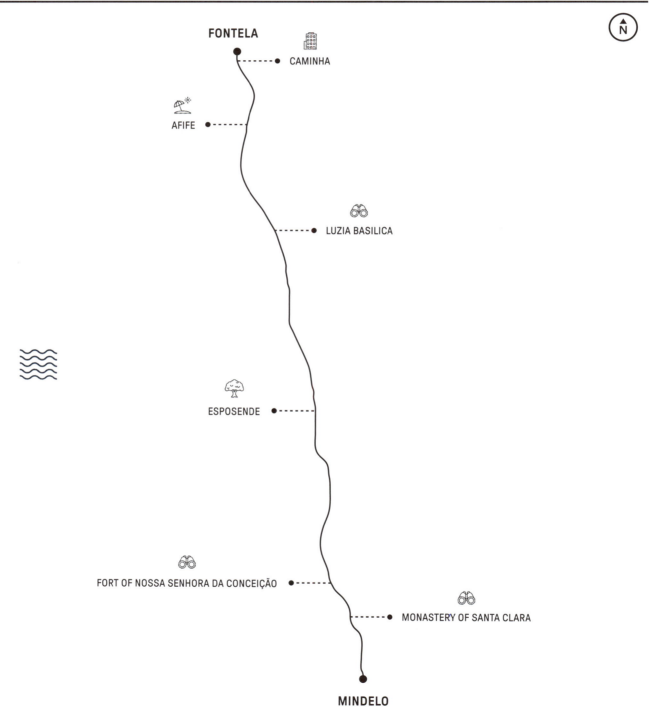

STAGE HIGHLIGHTS

 Caminha
Known for its medieval walls and the Matriz Church.

 Luzia Basilica
A hilltop basilica in Viana do Castelo, offering stunning views and beauty.

 Monastery of Santa Clara
Located in Vila do Conde, this historic monastery once was the biggest and wealthiest convent in the country.

 Fort of Nossa Senhora da Conceição
A coastal fort in Póvoa de Varzim, symbolising Portugal's old defenses.

Esposende Natural Park
A scenic hiking destination with diverse landscapes and the historic Esposende Defense Towers, round coastal fortifications built to protect the region.

Afife and Ofir Beaches
Pristine beaches offering excellent conditions for surfing.

Stage 73

MINDELO > SÃO JACINTO

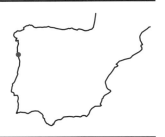

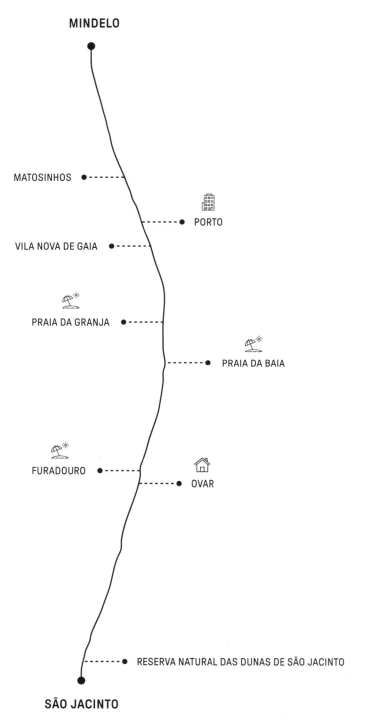

DATE	11/05/2023
DISTANCE	96.25 KM
ELEVATION	310 M
TOTAL TIME	15H12
MOVING TIME	13H09

SHOREHOLDERS
Igor Karpinski
Adrien Roose

STAGE HIGHLIGHTS

 Porto
The pearl of the stage, Norte's capital is built around the steep sides of the Douro River. Famous for its bridge designed by Gustave Eiffel's pupil, porto wine houses, steep narrow streets, a vibrant food scene, and one of the oldest bookstores in the world.

 Ovar
A charming inland town known for its azulejos, Portugal's famous decorative tiles, providing a cultural touch to the journey.

 Praia da Granja
One of Portugal's oldest seaside resorts, featuring elegant villas and wooden sidewalks, perfect for those seeking coastal charm and relaxation.

 Praia da Baia
A popular beach in Espinho, offering great waves for surfers and the chance to try your luck at the local casino.

 Praia do Furadouro
A paradise for windsurfers, offering thrilling conditions along Portugal's stunning coastline.

STAGE STORY

5.55 am. My phone buzzes with alerts: "Severe coastal event," "Major threat to human life." The forecast is ominous.

7.06 am. Max greets me with a warm smile that contrasts sharply with the cold, driving rain. He offers me his pro GoreTex jacket—an upgrade to my flimsy gear. I've never run more than a marathon, and now I'm staring down a storm. Protected by this magical layer, I feel ready. Let's do this.

7.41 am. The first photos show us smiling against the backdrop of towering 6 m waves. The rain is relentless, but the 85 km/h wind is mercifully at our side. Spirits are high; we can do this.

9.28 am. A quick coffee break with the crew. We refill bottles, wolf down tostas mistas, and hit the road. Porto awaits.

11.18 am. The wind eases, but the rain persists. I'm soaked through, and my lack of training is catching up. The thought of running three times this distance gnaws at me.

1.31 pm. My knee screams in pain, reducing me to a walk. Igor waits, visibly shaking with light hypothermia. At the next café, we pause. I can't see how I'll finish this.

3.01 pm. The rain stops, and we steel ourselves to continue. I try to run, but my IT band protests violently. Frustration and shame wash over me as I urge Igor to go on without me. The car arrives, and I'm on the verge of giving up. Desperate, I attempt running faster. The pain shifts, or maybe it's the caffeine. Either way, it's working.

3.40 pm. Coline joins us, then Chloe. Suddenly, the day brightens—literally and figuratively. The sun warms us, the pace is steady, and the finish line feels tangible.

6.58 pm. A final break. Max kneads our legs with expert precision, but my energy is fading fast. Darkness falls as we tackle the last stretch: 21 km through dunes and dense forest. We choose the forest.

7.16 pm. My legs give out again. Igor pushes ahead while I plan to stop at the next village. But in the maze of trees, we both get lost. The eerie stillness evokes the Blair Witch Project. We regroup, choosing the beach despite high tide and crashing waves. Flashlights dance over treacherous sand. It's risky, but there's no other way.

Miraculously, the beach widens. We're safe. A road appears, and I call it quits. I can barely stand, let alone run. It's been a grueling, extraordinary day—one I'll never forget.

Stage 74

SÃO JACINTO > COSTA NOVA

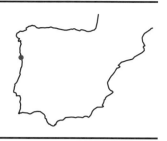

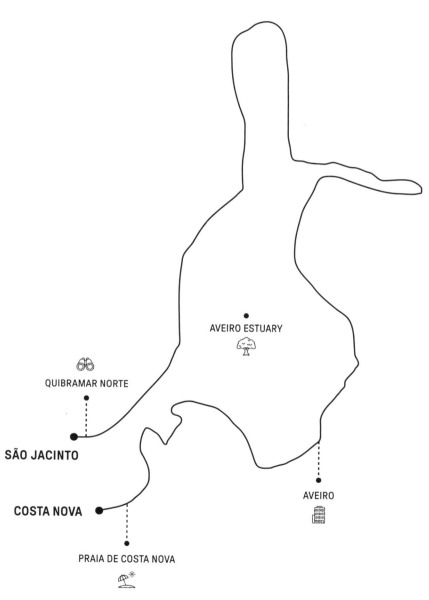

DATE	12/05/2023
DISTANCE	104.08 KM
ELEVATION	650 M
TOTAL TIME	13H09
MOVING TIME	11H41

SHOREHOLDER
Lars Hanegraaf

STAGE HIGHLIGHTS

A unique 100 km route where the start and finish are only 2 km apart, separated by the massive Aveiro estuary.

Aveiro
The finish is near the wonderful city of Aveiro, often called the "Venice of Portugal," which will be explored further in the Centro region chapter.

Quibramar Norte Lighthouse
The stage begins near this iconic lighthouse on the north bank of the Aveiro River.

Aveiro Estuary
A journey through wetlands and roads, rounding the expansive estuary due to the absence of bridges, offering a distinct landscape.

Praia de Costa Nova
The stage concludes on the pristine sands of Costa Nova, known for its vibrant striped houses and serene coastal charm.

STAGE STORY

Follow the coast... it seemed to me like an awesome initiative and while looking for my first ultrarunning experience it had to be this! Running the beaches at my own (relaxed) pace while being followed around by two dudes, with their dog, blasting music from a van, what could go wrong?

Arriving early morning at the beach of São Jacinto I could see the finish line already, only 2 km away - right across the bay! Little did I know of the 100 km of swamp and dust that awaited me.

The stage was dusty, the sun was out, the wind was strong, but the pace was good and before I knew it 20, 30, 40 km flew by. It wasn't until 50 km that it started to get a little rough. The trail had gone wild and was completely overgrown. Up through my neck in weeds and plants I pushed and clawed my way forward. "What took you so long? We thought you mentally broke, we didn't see you move on the map at all!" is what I heard meeting up with the support crew. Luckily that wasn't the case, and after downing a red bull I pushed on.

Endless dusty roads, swamps, sand and wind. Peaceful and quiet. This is how I would describe this stage. It felt quite remote when suddenly a small harbour or little village would show up out of nowhere.

After roughly 80-90 km the city of Aveiro appeared on the horizon and I knew I was close. The strong headwinds as I approached the harbour made it really difficult to progress, I nearly came to a standstill. Looking back, this is where I really started to struggle, but suddenly out of nowhere the now familiar van showed up in the distance and I was accompanied by AC/DC and Rage Against the Machine blasting next to me during a motivational drive by party. This helped me push on towards the final stretch of beach to the Costa Nova do Prado.

Just as the sun was setting I looked back and could again see the place where I started all those hours ago in the morning, just out of reach. In front of me... a delicious Duvel at the finish line.

↱ Regions 6 / 10
　　Centro

28,462 km²
2.3 million inhabitants

→ PRAIA DO NORTE, NAZARÉ

FAROL DO CABO MONDEGO

↳ Centro, the heart of Portugal, is a captivating region where historic charm and natural beauty intertwine. Stretching from the Atlantic coastline to the rugged Serra da Estrela mountains, Centro offers a diverse landscape of sandy beaches, rolling hills, and ancient forests.

Centro's moderate climate nurtures lush landscapes and fertile plains, perfect for vineyards and olive groves. Along the coast, dramatic cliffs and golden beaches provide a haven for surfers and sunseekers, while inland, peaceful rivers and thermal springs invite relaxation. The region's biodiversity, from oak forests to wetlands, supports a vibrant array of wildlife.

Home to the medieval university city of Coimbra, charming towns like Óbidos, and UNESCO World Heritage sites, Centro also boasts countless trails for hiking and cycling. It's a region where history, nature, and serenity meet, offering a truly authentic Portuguese experience.

Centro	150 km Coastline Captal: Coimbra

Centro
↳ Introduction

HOW TO GET AROUND

Centro is the third most populous region in Portugal, with 2 million inhabitants, located between the Norte region (with Porto as its capital) and the Lisbon region (with Lisbon as its capital). Unlike its neighbours, Centro features mid-sized cities, with Leiria and Coimbra being the largest.

International travellers can reach the region by flying into Porto or Lisbon, with a 3-hour drive on the A8 between the two extremities, allowing access to any destination within 1.5 hours by car when planned wisely.

WHERE TO STAY

The historic heart of Portugal, Coimbra is home to one of Europe's oldest universities, a UNESCO World Heritage site. The Joanina Library is a Baroque masterpiece, while the Chapel of São Miguel and the Royal Palace showcase the city's rich history. Stroll through the medieval streets of the old town, visit the Romanesque Sé Velha Cathedral, and enjoy Coimbra's vibrant cultural scene. Coimbra's fado music adds to its unique charm.

The sandy beaches with consistent waves attract many tourists looking to learn how to surf. You will find surf-oriented hotels and Airbnbs in destinations like Peniche, Figueira da Foz, Nazaré, Ericeira, or Silveira, offering surf sessions just a stroll away.

If you are looking for charm over water, Aveiro, São Martinho do Porto, or Costa Nova are all excellent options. Aveiro, known as the "Venice of Portugal," offers canals, colourful boats, while nearby Costa Nova boasts iconic striped houses. São Martinho do Porto is a serene village with a unique shell-shaped bay, offering calm waters ideal for families, making it perfect for a quiet getaway and scenic walks.

HISTORY

The Centro region of Portugal boasts a rich history shaped by ancient civilisations, medieval conflicts, and vibrant cultural traditions. Prehistoric evidence includes megalithic monuments and Roman settlements like the Conímbriga Ruins, showcasing advanced engineering and mosaics. During the Roman era, the region thrived as a hub of trade and agriculture, particularly in cities like Coimbra, then known as Aeminium.

The Moors brought significant advancements, including irrigation techniques and cultural influences, until the region was reclaimed by Christian forces during the Reconquista in the 12th century. Coimbra became Portugal's first capital in 1139, remaining a centre of political and cultural power. The establishment of the University of Coimbra in 1290 cemented its status as a beacon of learning.

The medieval walled town of Óbidos, gifted to Portuguese queens for centuries, adds a unique charm to the region. Known for its well-preserved streets, Gothic architecture and literary heritage, Óbidos also showcases Portugal's ceramic tradition. Vibrant tiles and handmade pottery from the Centro region reflect centuries of craftsmanship, blending Moorish and Iberian designs.

During the Age of Discoveries, Centro's fertile lands supported maritime expansion, and landmarks like the Batalha Monastery and the Convent of Christ in Tomar commemorate military and religious victories. Today, the Centro region preserves its legacy through historical sites and vibrant ceramics.

CENTRO

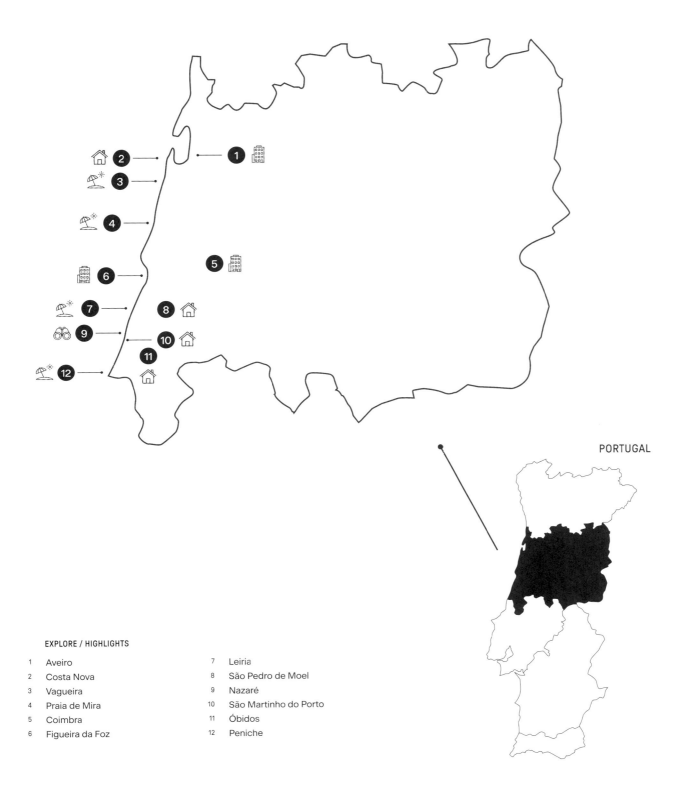

EXPLORE / HIGHLIGHTS

1. Aveiro
2. Costa Nova
3. Vagueira
4. Praia de Mira
5. Coimbra
6. Figueira da Foz
7. Leiria
8. São Pedro de Moel
9. Nazaré
10. São Martinho do Porto
11. Óbidos
12. Peniche

BALEAL

Centro
↳ Highlights

Portugal's Centro region boasts a stunning coastline rich in cultural and natural beauty. From the striped houses of Costa Nova to the canals of Aveiro, it's a blend of tradition and charm. The wild waves of Nazaré attract surfers chasing world record-breaking swells of more than 30 m in heigh, while Peniche offers golden beaches and more world-famed waves at the beach of Supertubos.

Nature lovers find charm in the Berlengas Islands, while serene bays like São Martinho do Porto contrast with dramatic cliffs and historic towns, creating a captivating coastal experience.

1. AVEIRO

Often referred to as the "Venice of Portugal" due to its canals and colourful moliceiro boats, Aveiro is a key city in the Centro region, celebrated for its unique charm, Art Nouveau architecture, and proximity to coastal gems like Costa Nova.

2. COSTA NOVA

Famous for its striped houses, Costa Nova is a picturesque village near Aveiro. Its long sandy beach is ideal for relaxing or enjoying water sports. The traditional moliceiro boats and nearby lagoon add to the charm of this unique coastal destination.

3. VAGUEIRA

Vagueira blends natural beauty with tradition, featuring fishermen using ancient xávega netting techniques. Its beach is a mix of golden sands and waves perfect for surfers. Nearby lagoons and pine forests offer opportunities for hiking and cycling.

4. PRAIA DE MIRA

Praia de Mira is a peaceful beach known for its golden sands and traditional wooden fishing boats. Its lagoons and nearby forests are perfect for hiking and birdwatching, while the beach itself is ideal for families seeking a laid-back experience.

5. COIMBRA

The historic heart of Portugal, Coimbra is home to one of Europe's oldest universities, a UNESCO site. The Joanina Library is a Baroque masterpiece, while the Chapel of São Miguel and the Royal Palace showcase rich history. Stroll through the medieval streets of the old town, visit the Romanesque Sé Velha Cathedral, and enjoy the city's vibrant cultural scene. Coimbra's fado music adds to its unique charm.

6. FIGUEIRA DA FOZ

This lively beach town features the expansive Praia da Claridade, perfect for sunbathing, surfing, and family outings. Its promenade, casino, and cultural attractions like the Santos Rocha Museum make it a well-rounded destination. The nearby Serra da Boa Viagem offers stunning coastal views.

7. LEIRIA

A short detour inland, Leiria boasts a magnificent medieval castle with sweeping views, charming old streets, and a lively cultural scene.

8. SÃO PEDRO DE MOEL

A picturesque seaside village with quaint charm, dramatic cliffs, and a lighthouse offering stunning views of the Atlantic.

9. NAZARÉ

Nazaré is world-famous for its giant waves, drawing surfers and spectators alike to Praia do Norte. Visit the Fort of São Miguel Arcanjo for views of the crashing waves and the surfers who conquer them. The village's traditional charm includes locals in colourful seven-layered skirts, fresh seafood, and vibrant festivals.

The biggest recorded wave in Nazaré was ridden by Sebastian Steudtner in 2024, measuring 28.57 m (93.73 ft), officially the largest wave ever surfed. The reason why the biggest waves in the world are recorded here is the Nazaré canyon, an underwater gorge stretching 230 km and plunging to depths of 5,000 m. It funnels Atlantic swells directly toward the coast, dramatically amplifying their size and energy.

10. SÃO MARTINHO DO PORTO

This serene town features a shell-shaped bay, offering calm waters perfect for families. Stroll along the promenade, enjoy fresh seafood, or take a relaxing dip in the sheltered bay. Its scenic beauty and tranquil vibe make it a favourite getaway.

11. ÓBIDOS

This medieval walled town enchants visitors with its cobblestone streets, whitewashed houses and vibrant bougainvillea. Once a royal wedding gift, this historic gem features landmarks like the Óbidos Castle and charming churches.

Known for its cultural festivals and traditional Ginjinha, a sour cherry liqueur, Óbidos also showcases exquisite ceramics, reflecting centuries of craftsmanship. Its preserved Gothic and Moorish influences make it a must-visit destination.

12. PENICHE

A haven for surfers, Peniche is known for Supertubos Beach, hosting international surf competitions. Explore the Peniche Fortress, a historical site, and take a boat trip to the Berlengas Islands, a marine reserve with crystal-clear waters, perfect for snorkelling and diving.

PRAIA DO NORTE, NAZARÉ

PRAIA DO NORTE, NAZARÉ

↙ ERMIDA DE SANTO ESTÊVÃO DO BALEAL

VIEW FROM PENICHE ON BALEAL ↘

↰ PRAIA DO BALEAL, SUL

PRAIA DO BALEAL, SUL ↳

Stage 75

COSTA NOVA > PEDRÓGÃO

DATE	13/05/2023
DISTANCE	100 KM
ELEVATION	1,030 M
TOTAL TIME	10H17
MOVING TIME	9H35

SHOREHOLDER
Charles Van Haverbeke

FAROL DO CABO MONDEGO

STAGE HIGHLIGHTS

The route is defined by unbroken stretches of sandy beaches, estuaries, and serene pine forests. Runners pass through quiet forests and hidden coves, immersing themselves in the unspoiled natural beauty of the coastline.

Aveiro
The stage begins in this vibrant town, known for its colourful moliceiro boats and picturesque canals, offering a lively start to the journey.

Costa Nova
Featuring its iconic striped houses, this charming area marks the transition from Aveiro's vibrancy to the tranquility of the coastline.

Praia da Mira
A charming beach known for its golden sands and traditional fishing huts.

Figueira da Foz
The stage's most bustling stop, a lively coastal city famed for its expansive beach and cosmopolitan vibe, offering a brief contrast to the serene journey.

Pedrógão
The stage concludes in this laid-back beach town.

STAGE STORY

My second stage. Together with Max, as founders, we set a duty to fill the gaps when people cancel. The runner doesn't choose the Stage, the Stage chooses the runner. Somehow, I only get the long sandy ones.

In the hinterland between Porto and Lisbon, the Atlantic coast drops vertically from north to south along an endless stretch of sand. Because of the high water, we soon opted for the wetland inlands—despite my cocky remark the day before: "Why would you not run on the beach if you follow the coast? Isn't that the point?" The direct, humbling, yet empowering part of ultrarunning. Long flat roads alongside canals. The start was tough as I combated decompression from another race days before. The wheels weren't spinning. But the beauty of ultra is that things change—they never last. You have to hold that belief firmly.

After a rough 20 km, I hit a long asphalt stretch, later turning into a grind under the high sun. I love it. A glazing gaze, mouth open, leaning in a trance. High on life.

I mark the marathon point alone, a bit lost in a semi-dune desert, the loose sand dragging on my pace. Marathon des Sables flashes by, and I find joy in this struggle too. Figueira da Foz marks the biggest city and the 75 km point. Before that, the only true elevation of the stage. Max stands ready with an espresso—a true delight. The caffeine kicks away the fatigue, injecting euphoria before the hills.

Follow the Coast is like life. Some parts are glorious beaches, true highlights for Instagram. Others are backstory industrial terrains—forgotten places, rusty metal, grass springing through cracks. We embrace them all.

After Figueira, a 20 km stretch of sand with limited support awaits. Fatigue waltzes over me like an avalanche in the warm sun. A figure with a dog hands me a Red Bull. Warm gratitude fills me—offering caffeine must be the purest form of friendship.

Pedrógão greets me from afar. My Garmin, which often calls me unproductive, points out that at 93 km, I'm not close to hitting three digits. Max greets me, but I refuse a hug and the Trojan-horsian decompression—my mind is set on 100 km.

The next 45 minutes, I zigzag against the wind, reducing its force as I learned while sailing. After a few back-and-forths, I return to P-town and finally get my salty hug from Max—my rock in all this. Lisbon, 8,000 km from our start, feels closer now.

Stage 76

PEDRÓGÃO > LAGOS DE ÓBIDOS

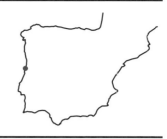

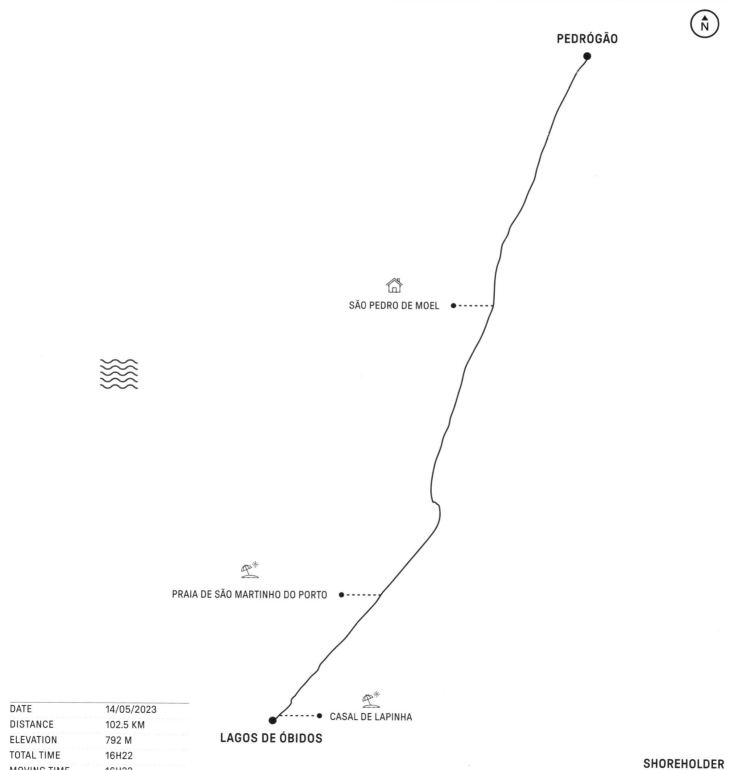

DATE	14/05/2023
DISTANCE	102.5 KM
ELEVATION	792 M
TOTAL TIME	16H22
MOVING TIME	16H22

SHOREHOLDER
Simon Corne

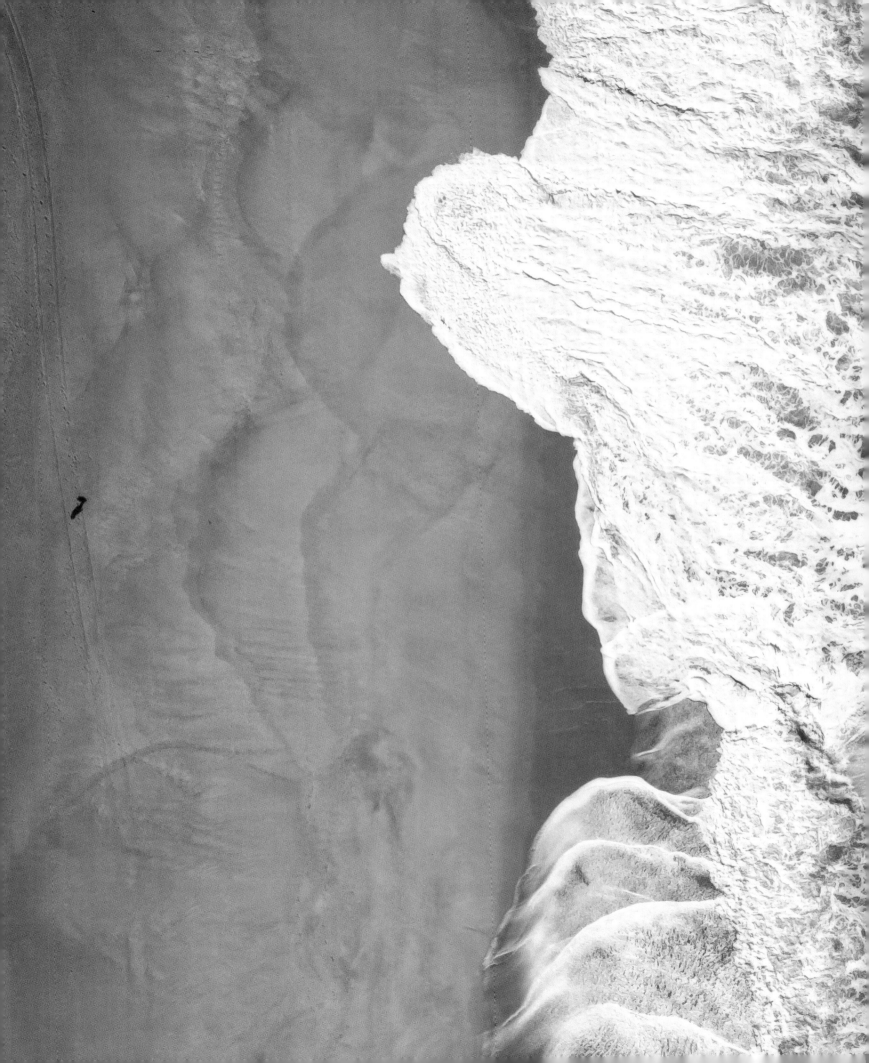

STAGE HIGHLIGHTS

We are entering surf country where consistent waves of the Atlantic hit the Portuguese shores.

 São Pedro de Moel
A charming village with quaint streets, a picturesque lighthouse, and a peaceful bay perfect for a short respite on the journey.

 São Martinho do Porto
Known for its unique shell-shaped bay, featuring calm waters embraced by rolling hills—a striking contrast to the rugged coastline.

 Nazaré
An iconic stop for surfers and thrill-seekers, famous for Praia do Norte and the world's largest surfable waves, created by the immense Nazaré Canyon beneath the ocean.

 Casal de Lapinha
The stage concludes near this coastal area, blending the tranquility of sandy shores with the rugged beauty of Portugal's dramatic coastline.

STAGE STORY

When I first met Charles, he shared his wild idea of organising a relay course along Europe's coastline. A few months later, Follow The Coast was born. I immediately felt drawn to the challenge. I love pushing my limits, so I decided to take the plunge and run a stage.

However, my journey wasn't smooth. After training alone for six months, I began experiencing intense stabbing pain in my lower back, which eventually spread to my neck. There were days I couldn't even get out of bed. But I was determined to reach my goal.

I saw three specialists, took painkillers, and went through four months of treatments with my physiotherapist, Nicolas. Eventually, my back was ready for action. But after months of inactivity, I had no stamina left, so I had to start from scratch.

I asked my friend Ubbie, a running coach, to guide me. With her help, I felt like I could take on anything. One month before my stage, I ran my first marathon. It wasn't the smartest idea. At 20 km, pain shot through my left knee, but I pushed through. I finished in 4 hours and 55 minutes and knew I was capable of completing my Follow the Coast stage.

The day of my stage arrived, and I was overwhelmed with emotion when my family came to support me. My nerves were high, but I focused on the task ahead.

The first 30 km were long and repetitive on empty beaches, but then the sun rose, the waves crashed, and birds flew overhead. I felt a deep sense of joy. The stage was tough with sandy stretches and dunes, but I kept going. At 50 km, my sister Ines and her boyfriend Vincent joined me, taking turns running with me. Their support made all the difference.

Around the 60 km mark, we faced a steep 30-m-high dune. It was a tough climb, but we fought our way to the top, laughing at the pain in our calves. The final 15 km were quieter, my body running on autopilot. With my dad by my side, I reflected on how he shaped me into who I am today.

I crossed the finish line in 16 hours and 22 minutes, tears streaming down my face. I sang, "Spread love like a Paddington bear!" My mom hugged me tightly, and I knew this wouldn't be my last stage.

Stage 77

LAGOS DE ÓBIDOS > AZENHAS DO MAR

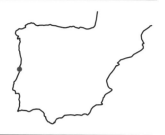
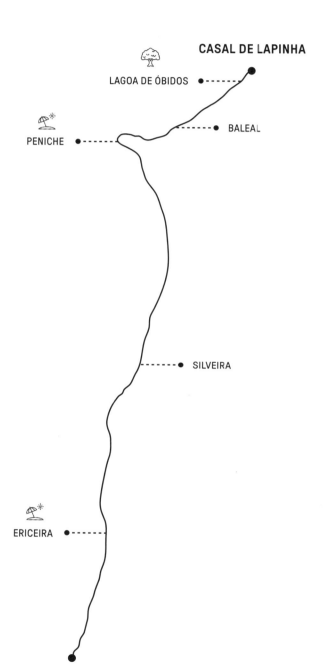

DATE	15/05/2023
DISTANCE	100.04 KM
ELEVATION	2,028 M
TOTAL TIME	9H31
MOVING TIME	9H27

SHOREHOLDER
Michiel Van Der Bauwhede

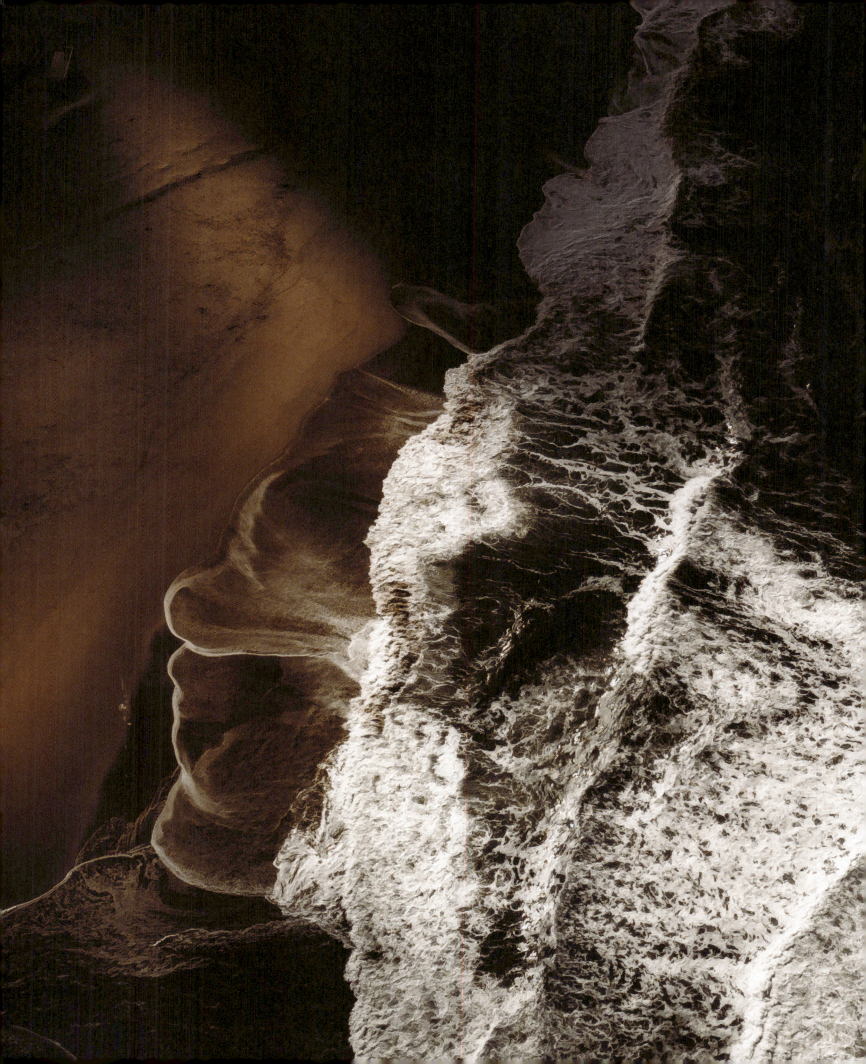

STAGE HIGHLIGHTS

This is THE stage for surfers. Peniche and Ericeira are viewed among the best spots in the world for waves.

Peniche
A peninsula offering year-round surf with beaches facing multiple directions. Supertubos, famous for its barrel-like waves, is a highlight, along with Baleal's picturesque surf spots and coastal views.

Ericeira
A cliffside town blending historic charm with a vibrant surf culture. Its beaches, tucked into bays, provide diverse surf conditions, complemented by inviting cafes and traditional Portuguese ambiance.

Óbidos
A fairy-tale medieval town featuring whitewashed houses, narrow cobbled streets, and a majestic castle, offering a serene and cultural detour.

Lagoa de Óbidos
A tranquil lagoon between Peniche and Óbidos, known for its birdlife and peaceful opportunities for exploration, providing balance to the dynamic coastal journey.

STAGE STORY

It was Monday, May 15th, 4 am. My alarm went off, signaling time for 200 grams of rice with brown sugar in a 4-star hotel room, while the buffet breakfast remained off-limits. A quick bite, then back to bed.

At 6 am, the second alarm rang. I grabbed a coffee and headed to the start line, meeting Max, a tired Lars, and an always cheerful Julien. This was it – Stage 77, from Casal de Lapinha to Azenhos do Mar. I was feeling confident after a solid marathon and had ambitiously set a goal to complete the stage in under 9 hours. (Spoiler: I took a wrong turn after 3 km, but who's counting?)

The run started off well under sunny skies. Julien paced us for the first 100 m, and I set a faster pace than planned – 4:45 min/km – running along the stunning Atlantic coastline. At 20 km, I left the sand and hit a gravel road. A small dog chased me, but it didn't faze me. The heat, however, started to build.

In Peniche, we took a brief detour for a drone shot. I felt awe and happiness, taking in the power of the ocean. But the clock was ticking. By marathon distance, those Maurten gels started making their presence known. I could barely stomach anything, but I kept my pace. Then, at kilometre 62, disaster struck. I hit a wall. I'd been overconfident, and now I was paying the price. The next 13 km were brutal. I felt empty, lost, and frustrated.

Then came the DAFCAF – not the original, but a cold, sweet red drink that saved me from despair. Reinvigorated, I let go of the 9-hour goal and focused on finishing. It was tough, insane even, but also one of the most rewarding experiences of my life.

As I crossed the "finish line," flanked by my wife Sara, Max, and Lars, I felt an unspoken connection with them. Strangers at the start of the day, now comrades in this incredible journey. I'll return year after year, coast by coast, because nothing compares to the feeling of crossing the finish line on a Follow The Coast stage.

*Dafcaf is a self-invented concept and acronym for the consumption of both dafalgan and caffeine in one consumption, which is ofte used to handle pain and fatigue in sport.

↪ Regions 7 / 10 3,015.24 km²
Lisbon 2,961,177 inhabitants

→ CABO ESPICHEL

MUSEU DE ARTE, ARQUITETURA E TECNOLOGIA, LISBON

↳ The Lisbon region, Portugal's vibrant heart, is a captivating blend of cultural heritage, coastal beauty, and urban sophistication. Nestled between the Atlantic Ocean and the rolling hills of central Portugal, this region offers a tapestry of experiences, from the historic charm of its towns to the contemporary energy of its capital.

Lisbon, the nation's capital, enchants with its cobbled streets, iconic trams, and panoramic viewpoints. Just beyond the city, the coastline unfolds with golden beaches and dramatic cliffs, making it a haven for surfers and sun-seekers. Inland, the region transitions into tranquil landscapes of olive groves, vineyards, and quaint villages.

This area is steeped in history and legend, from the fairy-tale palaces of Sintra to the maritime landmarks of Cascais and the windswept Cabo da Roca, mainland Europe's westernmost point. Rich in biodiversity, the region also includes natural parks, such as Arrábida, where lush hills meet turquoise waters.

Lisbon

240 km Coastline
Capital: Lisbon

Lisbon
↳ Introduction

HOW TO GET AROUND

Lisbon's airports is one of Europe's busiest airport offering on average 200 flights per day and hosting more than 30 million passengers.

The city of Lisbon can be covered by Uber, train or scooter but take into account its hilly shores when planning your day.

WHERE TO STAY

The city of Lisbon offers the lion share of accommodation in the region - with more than 700 hotels and more than 20,000 private owned rooms - making it a great launch pad for any activities in the region.

All highlights, including the most Northern Azenhas do Mar and the most southern Cabo Espichel are within 1 hour driving range.

HISTORY

Lisbon, Portugal's vibrant capital, is a city of contrasts where historic charm meets modern energy. As one of Europe's oldest cities, founded around 1200 BCE by the Phoenicians, it has been shaped by a rich history of conquest and resilience. Occupied by the Romans, it became a flourishing trading hub, later falling to the Moors, who influenced its architecture and culture for over 400 years. The Christians reclaimed it during the Reconquista in 1147, ushering in a period of growth.

Lisbon was a key player in Portugal's Age of Discoveries, serving as the launch point for explorers like Vasco da Gama, whose voyage to India in 1498 transformed global trade. Landmarks like Belém Tower and Jerónimos Monastery, both UNESCO sites, commemorate this golden era. The 1755 earthquake, one of Europe's most devastating natural disasters, reshaped the city, leading to the construction of the grand Baixa Pombalina, a pioneering example of earthquake-resistant urban planning.

Lisbon's cobblestone streets wind through neighbourhoods like Alfama, the city's oldest district, known for its fado music, narrow alleys, and Moorish influences. The iconic Tram 28 offers a scenic ride past landmarks such as São Jorge Castle, once a Moorish fort, and Praça do Comércio, a grand riverside square.

Beyond the city, the surrounding areas reflect this layered history. Sintra, a UNESCO site, showcases royal palaces like the Pena Palace and the mysterious Quinta da Regaleira, blending Romantic and Gothic influences. The dramatic cliffs of Cabo da Roca mark the westernmost point of mainland Europe. Coastal towns like Cascais and Carcavelos provide sandy beaches and chic promenades, while Costa da Caparica attracts surfers with its endless shores. Lisbon and its surroundings seamlessly blend history, nature, and culture, offering something for everyone.

LISBON

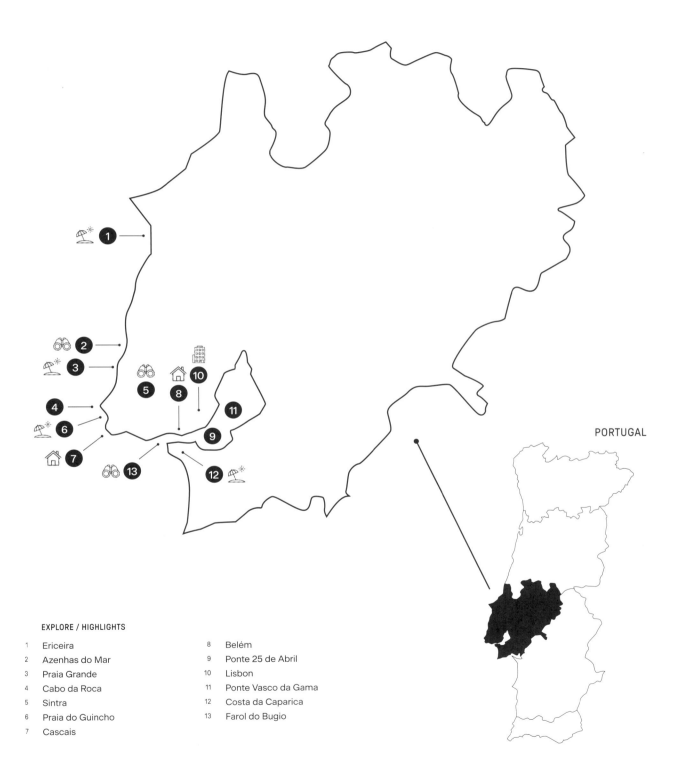

EXPLORE / HIGHLIGHTS

1. Ericeira
2. Azenhas do Mar
3. Praia Grande
4. Cabo da Roca
5. Sintra
6. Praia do Guincho
7. Cascais
8. Belém
9. Ponte 25 de Abril
10. Lisbon
11. Ponte Vasco da Gama
12. Costa da Caparica
13. Farol do Bugio

REGION 7 / 10

CABO DA ROCA

Lisbon
↳ Highlights

The Lisbon region offers an incredible mix of culture and nature. Lisbon's narrow streets are filled with the history of the early conquerors, colourful azulejos and an bustling food scene. Sintra's lush, green hills are dotted with colourful Moorish castles overseeing the area.

Those hills extend to the Atlantic coast, forming dramatic cliffs, of which Cabo Roca, the most Western point of Europe, is topped a proud lighthouse. Long stretches of beach add a touch of LA to Europe's most southern capital and surfers find the shores of Ericeira one of the best surf destinations in the world.

1. ERICEIRA

This charming fishing village is a global surfing mecca and one of the world's first World Surfing Reserve. Its beaches, like Ribeira d'Ilhas, offer world-class waves for surfers of all levels.

Beyond the surf, Ericeira captivates with cobblestone streets, whitewashed houses and fresh seafood restaurants. Its laid-back atmosphere, stunning cliffs, and Atlantic views make it a favourite for both adventure seekers and those looking for a relaxing escape.

2. AZENHAS DO MAR

This picturesque village near Sintra clings dramatically to cliffs overlooking the Atlantic. Its whitewashed houses cascade down toward a natural seawater pool, creating a postcard-perfect setting.

Known for its stunning views, this charming spot offers a blend of tradition and natural beauty. Visitors can explore winding streets, enjoy fresh seafood at cliffside restaurants, or simply marvel at the sunset over the ocean. A serene escape, rich in coastal charm.

3. PRAIA GRANDE

Nestled in Sintra's dramatic coastline, Praia Grande is a haven for surfers and families. Its expansive sandy shore is perfect for sunbathing, while its powerful waves attract surf enthusiasts.

The beach is also known for dinosaur footprints embedded in the cliffs, offering a glimpse into ancient history. With nearby cafes and easy access, Praia Grande combines natural beauty with a vibrant beach atmosphere.

4. CABO DA ROCA

The westernmost point of mainland Europe, this dramatic cape near Sintra comprises cliffs towering 140 m (460 ft) above the Atlantic Ocean. Offering breathtaking views, it's marked by a lighthouse and a monument inscribed with Luís de Camões' poetic words.

Nearby, scenic trails like the Rota Vicentina and Praia da Ursa hike wind through the Sintra-Cascais Natural Park, offering stunning landscapes of rugged cliffs, hidden beaches, and wildflower-covered hills. Perfect for nature lovers and adventurers.

5. SINTRA

A UNESCO World Heritage site, Sintra is a magical town known for its fairytale-like palaces and lush landscapes. Nestled in the hills, highlights include the colourful Pena Palace, the mysterious Quinta da Regaleira with its spiral well, and the medieval Moorish Castle.

Surrounded by the Sintra-Cascais Natural Park, it offers scenic trails and ocean views. Rich in history and charm, Sintra blends architectural wonders with a romantic, mystical atmosphere, making it a must-visit destination.

6. PRAIA DO GUINCHO

Located near Cascais, Praia do Guincho is famed for its wild beauty and strong winds, making it a top spot for windsurfing and kitesurfing. Backed by rolling dunes and the Serra de Sintra, this beach offers a dramatic setting for outdoor enthusiasts. Its unspoiled nature, combined with proximity to Cascais' luxury amenities, makes Guincho a favourite for adventure and relaxation alike.

PONTE 25 DE ABRIL, LISBON

FARO DO CABO ESPICHEL

7. CASCAIS

Located to the east of the capital, this charming seaside town is known for its elegant promenades, sandy beaches and vibrant marina. Once a royal retreat, it boasts cultural gems like the Citadela fortress and Boca do Inferno cliffs. A blend of history, luxury, and natural beauty, Cascais is perfect for relaxation and exploration.

8. BELÉM

This historic district in Lisbon is known for its maritime heritage and iconic landmarks. Visit the Belém Tower, a symbol of Portugal's Age of Discoveries, and the Jerónimos Monastery, a UNESCO site. Don't miss the Monument to the Discoveries and the famous Pastéis de Belém café. The riverside setting and rich history make it a must-see.

9. PONTE 25 DE ABRIL

Lisbon's iconic suspension bridge spans the Tagus River, linking Lisbon to Almada. Resembling San Francisco's Golden Gate, it offers stunning views of the city and the Cristo Rei statue. Completed in 1966, it's a vital connection and a symbol of Lisbon's modernity and progress.

10. LISBON

Portugal's vibrant capital city offers a mix of history, culture and modern charm. Explore its azulejo-clad streets, jump aboard one of its historic trams, and visit landmarks such as the hilltop São Jorge Castle and Belém Tower.

Enjoy panoramic views from one of the many miradouros (viewpoints), a thriving food scene, and the waterfront vibes along the Tagus River. A city of endless discovery.

11. PONTE VASCO DA GAMA

Europe's longest bridge at 17 km, this cable-stayed bridge connects Lisbon to Montijo. Opened in 1998, it is named after the Portuguese explorer and nobleman who was the first European to reach India by sea. Its sleek design and engineering marvel blend seamlessly with the estuary's natural beauty, offering stunning views and efficient transport.

12. COSTA DA CAPARICA

This long stretch of golden beaches backed by dunes and pine forests is popular for its surfing and beach bars. The coastal boardwalks, stunning cliffs, Atlantic views and nearby fishing village charm visitors, making the area a favourite getaway for locals and tourists alike.

13. FAROL DO BUGIO

This iconic lighthouse in the Tagus River estuary sits on the Fort of São Lourenço do Bugio, a circular 17th-century fort built to defend Lisbon. Blending history and engineering, the striking structure guiding ships safely into the harbour.

Accessible only by boat, it offers a fascinating view of maritime heritage against the backdrop of Lisbon's skyline. Bugio stands as a symbol of resilience, enduring centuries of tides and storms while guarding the Portuguese capital.

NAZARÉ

TEJO, LISBON

↰ RAÇA DO COMÉRCIO, LISBON

TORRE DE BELEM, LISBON ↲

PADRÃO DOS DESCOBRIMENTOS, LISBON

CABO DA ROCA

CABO ESPICHEL · CABO ESPICHEL

Stage 78

AZENHAS DO MAR > SAMORA CORREIA

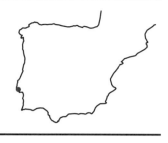

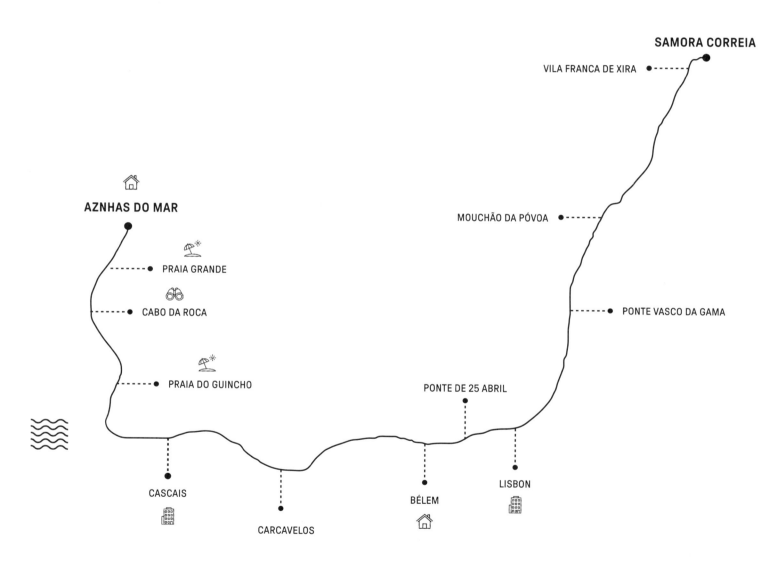

DATE	16/05/2023
DISTANCE	100.59 KM
ELEVATION	870 M
TOTAL TIME	15H58
MOVING TIME	14H16

SHOREHOLDERS
Lode Van Laere
Wim Christiaens

PRAÇA DO COMÉRCIO, LISBON

STAGE HIGHLIGHTS

 Azenhas do Mar
A picturesque village perched on rugged cliffs, with whitewashed houses offering stunning views of the Atlantic Ocean.

 Cascais
A sophisticated seaside town, renowned for its luxury resorts & relaxed charm.

 Belém
A historic area in Lisbon, home to iconic landmarks like the Jerónimos Monastery and the Ponte 25 de Abril suspension bridge.

 Lisbon
Portugal's vibrant capital blending history, culture, and charm.

 Cabo da Roca
Europe's westernmost point, featuring dramatic coastlines.

 Praia Grande and Guincho
Beaches known for their powerful waves, making them hotspots for surfers.

 Tejo Estuary
A tranquil haven for birdlife and nature enthusiasts.

STAGE STORY

We're excited to share our story as new shoreholders in the Follow The Coast adventure! We're Lode and Wim, and we had the privilege of running the Lisbon stage—a day that turned out to be an unforgettable mix of challenges, triumphs, and laughter.

The adventure held extra meaning for Lode, who celebrated his 40th birthday that morning. The day began on a high note as two friends surprised him by joining us, alongside another close friend who lives in Lisbon. The first 20 km were a surprising test of endurance, as the trail from Sintra to Cascais revealed itself to be steep and rugged, more of a mountain adventure than a coastal jog. The dramatic cliffs and lush surroundings, however, made every step worth it.

Once the trail levelled out, we faced an entirely different beast: heat. The temperature soared to an unforgiving 36°C, a stark contrast to the cooler 15°C days we had trained in. The relentless sun tested our limits, but the beautiful Lisbon beaches and their vibrant atmosphere provided welcome distractions. A few kind souls along the route even cheered us on, boosting our spirits when we needed it most.

The day wasn't without its rough patches. By kilometre 60, Lode's energy gave out, and he had a brief but dramatic encounter with the ground—passing out next to an unceremonious pile of his own vomit. Fortunately, after a quick recovery, he was back on his feet, albeit a little less glamorous than when we'd started.

Despite the heat, exhaustion, and challenges, we couldn't be prouder of the experience. Running this stage not only pushed our limits but also deepened our appreciation for Portugal's stunning coastline and the supportive spirit of the Follow The Coast community. Looking back, we wouldn't change a thing—well, maybe the vomit part!

Stage 79

SAMORA CORREIA > VERDERENA

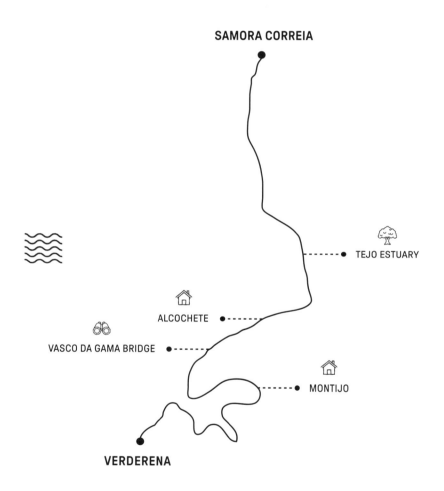

DATE	17/05/2023
DISTANCE	88 KM
ELEVATION	466 M
TOTAL TIME	13H17
MOVING TIME	12H54

SHOREHOLDER
Gaetan D'Hondt

STAGE HIGHLIGHTS

A harmonious mix of engineering feats, serene villages, and unique wildlife, showcasing the beauty of the Tagus.

 Alcochete and Montijo
Charming riverside villages with quaint streets, peaceful retreats, and welcoming atmospheres.

 Tejo Estuary
A scenic stage along vast salt marshes and winding riverbeds, blending natural beauty with tranquil landscapes. A paradise for bird enthusiasts, with options to explore the estuary's rich biodiversity by boat for an up-close experience.

 Vasco da Gama Bridge
Europe's longest bridge, spanning 17 km across the Tagus River, an engineering marvel and modern contrast to the estuary.

STAGE STORY

It's May 17th, 2023, at 7 a.m. I stand at a lonely Repsol station in the heart of Lisbon Bay. After a warm welcome and blessing from Max, I set off, running a straight line along a national road. The industrial surroundings were far from the idyllic landscapes other Shoreholders had enjoyed. But after navigating those treacherous first 16 km, I finally reached country roads. The landscape felt like the American Midwest—a surprising twist.

When registering for the stage, I envisioned running through the Tagus River delta. In reality, most of it was private farmland. Fortunately, my dad had rented a gravel bike to accompany me. Unfortunately, he punctured his tire at the worst possible time: just as I ran out of water. The next 5 km were a dusty, dry struggle, until I finally reached Max and Lars for a much-needed refill. Refreshed and satisfied with my pace, I pressed on under the steadily warming sun.

I reached Alcochete, a peaceful village of whitewashed houses, with Lisbon visible across the river. The contrast between the tranquil village and the bustling city only 11 km away was striking. From there, I hit the Salinas do Samouco beaches—a true Follow the Coast moment. With my first marathon done, I felt euphoric, bouncing across the sand.

Passing under the Vasco da Gama Bridge, I saw the natural reserve's fence looming ahead. Forced to retrace my steps, I got an unexpected reprieve when Max informed me the park guard had granted permission to continue through the reserve. Climbing the fence, I found myself surrounded by stunning salt beds, flamingos, and breathtaking wildlife—a surreal highlight.

Back on asphalt, the heat soared to over 30°C. Passing through military zones and trash-filled deltas, I pushed forward, counting down the kilometres. My dad rejoined me after repairing his puncture, bringing much-needed supplies. At the 90 km mark, I faced the final stretch. Through towns, farmland, and a hauntingly impoverished stilt-house community, I trudged on.

Finally, the sound of the motivational van party propelled me to the finish line. After retracing muddy steps and climbing a wall due to a last-minute navigation error, I reached Terminal Rodo-Ferro-Fluvial do Barreiro. There was my reward: a Duvel, my dad, and the best support crew imaginable. Exhausted, I vowed never to do this again—but here I am, training for Stage 2. See you soon!

Stage 80

VERDERENA > PRAIA DO INFERNO

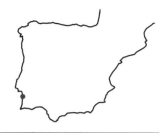

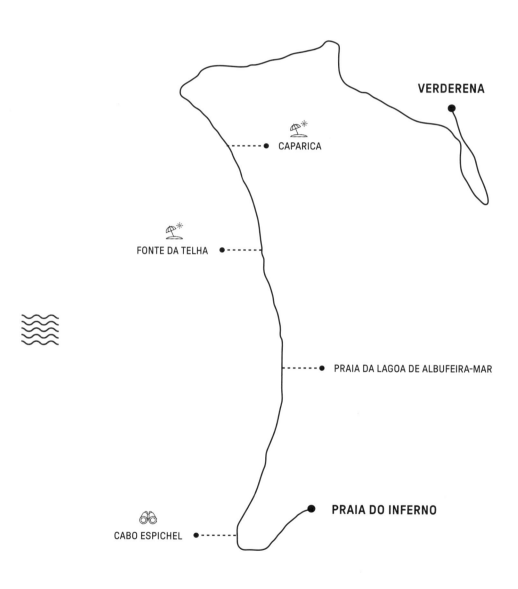

DATE	18/05/2023
DISTANCE	100.11 KM
ELEVATION	1,113 M
TOTAL TIME	13H24
MOVING TIME	11H39

SHOREHOLDER
Max Monteyne

CABO ESPICHEL

STAGE HIGHLIGHTS

A journey from industrial edges to tranquil beaches and awe-inspiring headlands, celebrating Portugal's coastal beauty.

Caparica and Fonte da Telha
Golden sandy beaches draw visitors with endless stretches of sun, surf, and vibrant holiday energy. While Caparica brings LA vibes with its many modern beach bars, Fonte da Telha has the spirit of a desolate cowboy town, much closer to nature.

Sado Estuary
A scenic transition to tranquil waters and rich ecosystems, offering a serene break along the southern coastline.

Cabo Espichel
Dramatic cliffs and sweeping ocean views create a natural highlight, adding grandeur to this stunning coastal journey.

STAGE STORY

Stage 80 wasn't just any stage—it marked the finale of our 2023 leg, a milestone of 8,000 km since our journey began in 2019, and a stunning run with Lisbon as its dramatic backdrop. After 1,700 km over three weeks, I stood at the start of this stage, utterly drained. Offering support for other runners had left me with little rest and even less training.

The run began, and by 12 km, I hit an unusual high—much too early for a 100 km day. Unsurprisingly, reality struck at kilometre 16, where the first crushing wave of fatigue hit, leaving me desperate to quit. The uneventful suburban scenery didn't help, with nothing to distract me until I approached the Ponte 25 de Abril and the iconic Cristo Rei statue. The climb to the statue was gruelling, and at only 30 km in, my body was screaming for relief.

Things shifted when I caught sight of the ocean again. After nearly 200 km along the Tagus Bay, the salty air and endless horizon gave me a much-needed boost. But the euphoria was short-lived. Passing through makeshift favelas with barefoot children was a stark reminder of inequality, leaving me unsettled and guilty as I continued my run equipped with modern gear.

At the beach, a gruelling stretch awaited me: 35 km of sand, half of it deserted and surreal. The high tide left me running on steep, compacted sand near the waterline, my right foot always landing lower than my left. The horizon refused to change no matter how fast—or slow—I moved. It felt like running through time itself.

Relief came when Charles, my inspiration and friend, joined me for the final 20 km. We began with a punishing dune climb, but his presence lifted my spirit. As the sun began to set, we reached Cabo Espichel, an awe-inspiring site with its monastery, lighthouse, and cliffs towering 200 m above the crashing Atlantic. The golden light, my friends cheering, and the monumental milestone of 8,000 km created a transcendent moment.

Running those last steps with Charles felt like flying. Through rocks, trails, and even a herd of sheep, we charged toward the finish line, powered by the collective effort of all the runners who had come before. As I crossed the finish, my parents, Simon, and Lars were there to celebrate.

The day ended with more than an emotional victory—we took Lisbon by storm, partying until 4 a.m. The post-run celebration made my legs feel rejuvenated, and the memory of that stage will forever be etched in my heart. It wasn't just a run; it was a testament to what's possible when passion and community collide.

↪ Regions 8 / 10
Alentejo

31,567 km²
537,556 inhabitants

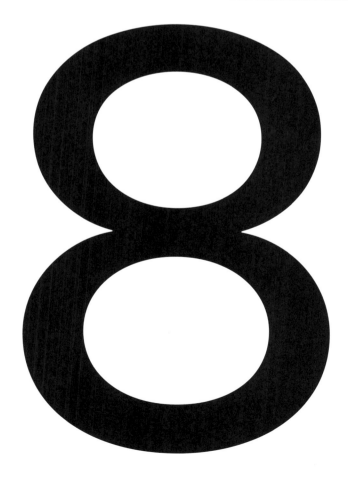

→ MALHÃO

↳ Alentejo, Portugal's largest region, enchants with golden plains, vineyards, and whitewashed villages. Known for cork trees, storks, olive groves, and rich gastronomy, it offers serene tranquillity.

Explore Évora's UNESCO heritage, ancient fortresses, and pristine beaches along a rugged coastline. The coastline divides into three parts. First, Setúbal's coast features dramatic cliffs, beaches, and turquoise waters, part of Arrábida Natural Park, extending to the Troía Peninsula—perfect for nature lovers and adventurers. Second, the Sado Estuary, a biodiverse area teeming with wildlife, from migratory birds to dolphins, making it a peaceful haven for nature enthusiasts and birdwatchers.

Third, the long stretch of beach near Comporta, Carvalhal, and Melides, where unspoiled sands and luxury resorts crafted by top architects create a sophisticated retreat. Comporta, now attracting the affluent, blends elegance with nature in an idyllic coastal paradise.

Alentejo

150 km Coastline
Capital: Évora

Alentejo
↳ Introduction

HOW TO GET THERE

For most international travellers, the best way to reach Alentejo is through nearby airports located just outside the region. Lisbon's Humberto Delgado Airport (LIS), positioned to the north, serves as the main gateway and is only a 1-2-hour drive from northern towns like Évora. For those heading to the southern parts of Alentejo, Faro Airport (FAO) in the Algarve is a convenient choice, with a similar 1-2-hour drive to coastal destinations such as Sines and Comporta.

WHERE TO STAY

Portugal's largest and most tranquil region, Alentejo is known for its authenticity and slower pace of life, and offers a rich tapestry of history, culture, and nature.

You will not find big cities here. The largest metropolitan areas include Évora, Beja, Portalegre, and Sines. This book also includes Setúbal and Sesimbra, known for their lush hills and coastal views.

Setúbal, a vibrant coastal city, blends history, culture, and natural beauty. Explore the Fort of São Filipe for panoramic views, enjoy fresh seafood at the Livramento Market, and visit the Church of Jesus, a Manueline gem. Nearby, the Arrábida Natural Park offers pristine beaches, while the Tróia Peninsula invites dolphin watching and beach relaxation. Known for its wine and traditional festivals, Setúbal is a dynamic destination where urban charm meets nature's allure.

Sines, a major industrial and port city on the coast, is famously known as the birthplace of Vasco da Gama. It offers a mix of history and modern infrastructure.

Head inland to visit Évora, a UNESCO World Heritage city perched on a hill overlooking cork tree groves, is the cultural and administrative capital of Alentejo. It's known for its Roman Temple, medieval cathedral, and rich history.

A regional agricultural hub, Beja is a historic city with roots in Roman and Moorish times. Its landmarks include a 13th-century hilltop castle, Pre-Romanesque churches and the Roman ruins of Pisões, an urban villa dating from the 1st century.

Nestled near the Serra de São Mamede, Portalegre is a picturesque city with a charming old town, baroque architecture and a textile heritage.

HISTORY

The history of Alentejo and the Setúbal area reflects a rich cultural tapestry. Inhabited since the Neolithic era, the region boasts megalithic monuments like the Almendres Cromlech and Roman sites such as Évora and Cetóbriga, which were pivotal in trade and salt production.

The Moors introduced advanced agricultural techniques and left a lasting architectural influence. During the Reconquista, Christian forces reclaimed the region, and towns like Elvas became key defensive strongholds, while Setúbal flourished as a hub for fishing and salt trade.

During the Age of Discoveries, Setúbal and Sines, the birthplace of Vasco da Gama, played significant roles in Portugal's maritime expansion. Alentejo became Portugal's breadbasket, producing wheat, cork, and olives, while Setúbal industrialised, exporting wine and canned fish.

Today, Alentejo's rich heritage, unspoiled landscapes, and Setúbal's blend of industry, tourism, and natural beauty continue to captivate visitors.

ALENTEJO

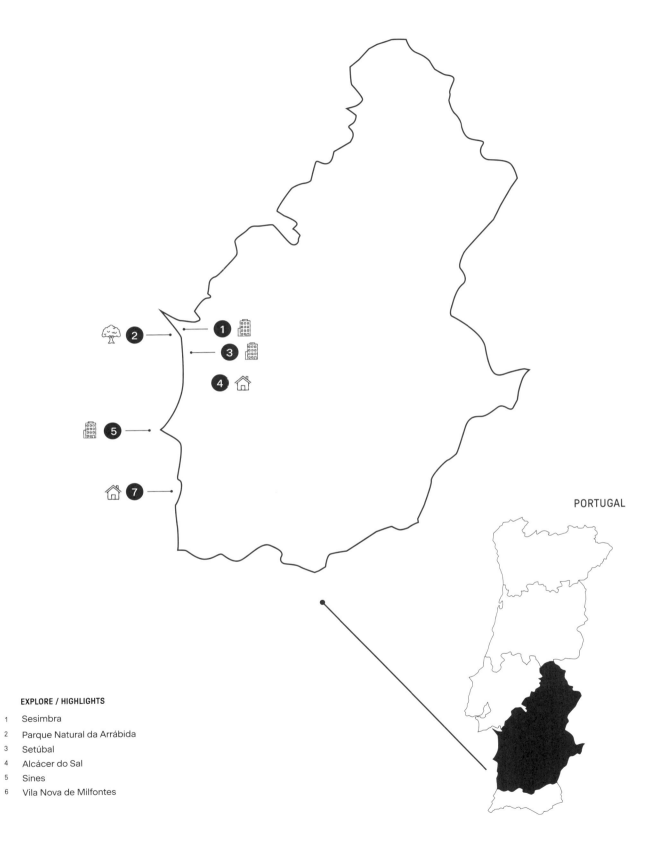

PORTUGAL

EXPLORE / HIGHLIGHTS

1. Sesimbra
2. Parque Natural da Arrábida
3. Setúbal
4. Alcácer do Sal
5. Sines
6. Vila Nova de Milfontes

PRAIA DA MALHA DA COSTA, COMPORTA

Alentejo
↳ Highlights

The Alentejo region, often called Portugal's serene heart, is a picturesque blend of rolling plains, historic charm, and rural traditions. Stretching from the Tagus River to the Algarve, it boasts golden fields, vineyards, and quaint whitewashed villages.

Évora, a UNESCO World Heritage site, captivates with Roman ruins, medieval architecture, and lively squares, while the unspoiled coastline offers tranquil beaches and rugged cliffs. Rich in history and flavour, Alentejo is famed for its robust wines, hearty cuisine, and ancient landmarks like megalithic monuments. It's a place to unwind and connect with nature's timeless beauty.

1. SESIMBRA

Just 30 minutes south of Lisbon, this fishing town boasts a lively harbour, beautiful beaches like Praia do Ouro, and access to the Lapa de Santa Margarida, a sea cave with a chapel.

2. ARRABIDA NATURAL PARK

Located near Setúbal, this stunning park with lush hills, limestone cliffs, and hidden beaches is perfect for hiking, swimming, and picnicking. Beaches include Praia dos Coelhos and Praia da Figueirinha, as well as Praia da Galapinhos, which is often celebrated as one of Portugal's most beautiful beaches.

Nestled against a backdrop of lush green hills, Praia da Galapinhos offers a serene escape with its soft golden sands and crystal-clear turquoise waters. This tranquil cove is perfect for swimming and snorkelling. Access requires a short hike down a well-marked trail, adding to its secluded charm. A must-visit for those seeking unspoiled beauty and a peaceful retreat.

3. SETÚBAL

A vibrant coastal city, Setúbal blends history, culture, and nature. Explore the charming old town, the bustling fish market, and the stunning views from São Filipe Fortress. A gateway to Arrábida Natural Park, it offers pristine beaches, hiking trails, and dolphin-watching tours in the Sado Estuary.

4. ALCÁCER DO SAL

This historic town on the Sado River is steeped in charm. Once a Moorish stronghold, it boasts a medieval castle offering panoramic views. Stroll along the riverside, explore cobbled streets, and enjoy fresh seafood. Nearby rice fields and nature reserves add to its allure.

5. SINES

This historic coastal town blends charm and industry as Portugal's largest artificial port. The birthplace of Vasco da Gama, it features a hilltop castle and a vibrant marina. The old town offers cobbled streets and cultural festivals, while nearby beaches like São Torpes attract surfers and sunseekers alike.

6. VILA NOVA DE MILFONTES

This charming town sits on the banks of the Mira River and boasts a relaxed vibe. Visit Praia das Furnas for a mix of river and ocean waters, ideal for families. Don't miss the Forte de São Clemente, a 17th-century fortress offering views of the estuary.

PRAIA DO MALHÃO

↰ MARINA DE TROIA, COMPORTA

MARINA DE TROIA, COMPORTA

↶ ARRABIDA NATURAL PARK

TROIA PENINSULA, COMPORTA ↷

↰ PRAIA DO CREIRO

FORTE DE SANTA MARIA DA ARRÁBIDA ↴

Stage 81

PRAIA DO INFERNO > GAMBIA

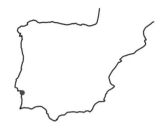

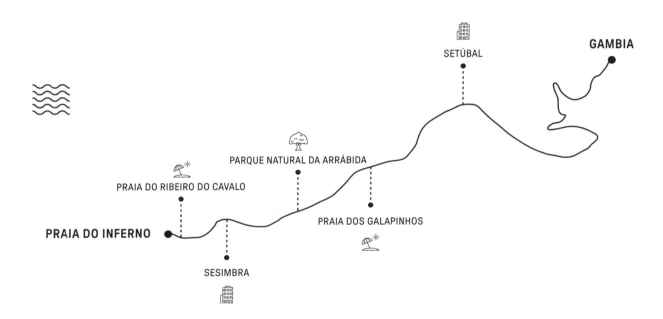

SHOREHOLDER
Cédric Spaas

7ª BATARIA DE COSTA, SETUBAL

STAGE HIGHLIGHTS

 Setúbal
A lively town renowned for its maritime heritage, vibrant atmosphere, and delicious seafood. The nearby Sado estuary is home to a resident population of bottlenose dolphins, offering the chance to spot them on a boat tour.

 Sesimbra
A charming coastal town offering beautiful beaches, fresh seafood, and a lively marina. Dolphin-watching tours often depart from here, giving visitors a chance to see them up close.

 Parque Natural da Arrábida
A stunning natural park featuring dramatic cliffs, lush forests, and panoramic ocean views. Dolphins are often spotted offshore, adding an extra touch of magic to the stunning vistas.

 Praia dos Galapinhos
One of Portugal's most picturesque beaches, with crystal-clear waters and a serene atmosphere. Its calm surroundings are occasionally visited by dolphins, making it a special stop.

 Praia do Ribeiro do Cavalo
Hidden and deserted beach with dramatic rocks, only accessible by a technical single trail.

Stage 82

GAMBIA > MOITINHA

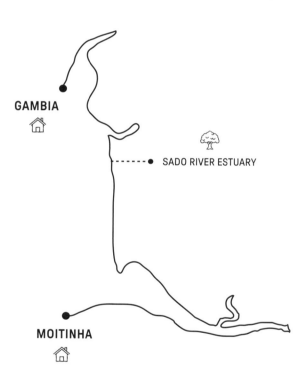

DATE	08/03/2024
DISTANCE	93.38 KM
ELEVATION	993 M
TOTAL TIME	14H07
MOVING TIME	11H46

SHOREHOLDERS

Ben Swerts
Olivier Wuyts
Céline Vervinckt
Pieterjan Van Leemputten

RICE FIELDS, COMPORTA

STAGE HIGHLIGHTS

Gambia
A small coastal town where this stage begins. Known for its proximity to the Sado River, it offers a quiet starting point before the route moves inland toward the estuary.

Sado River Estuary
A significant part of the Sado River Natural Park, this estuary is a vast wetland ecosystem teeming with birdlife, including flamingos and storks. The area is known for its lush vegetation, marshy landscapes, and serene beauty.

Moitinha
A small settlement near the coast marking the end of the stage. As the route approaches Moitinha, the landscape transitions from wetlands to coastal terrain, providing a mix of river and ocean views.

STAGE STORY

For some of us, it was our first time tackling an ultra-run. To fuel our motivation and make a difference, we linked our effort to a good cause. This passion paid off, as we managed to raise an astounding €40,000 for the Olivia Fund!

The Follow The Coast project promotes beach cleanliness by running along European shores. For Stage 82, we expected beaches and ocean views but instead faced the Sado River estuary's marshy wetlands—no sea in sight. Despite this, it was just us, our team, and the journey ahead!

The day started sunny and full of energy, though the unpredictability of the course became clear early on when we encountered an impassable pedestrian bridge. Yet, from the first kilometre, the atmosphere was electric. Four runners who were initially friends of friends quickly bonded over shared laughter, encouragement, and mental support—aided, of course, by plenty of energy gels.

Our incredible support crew deserves special mention. From delivering supplies and dry socks to cheering us on, they were the glue holding us together. Among them was the youngest and cutest supporter, Benoît-Victor, son of Ben and Sofie, only weeks old but already an inspiration with his smile.

At 50 km, the challenge escalated when one of our team members sustained an injury. Though unable to continue, they became a super-supporter, walking further than planned to cheer us on. As fatigue set in, dense bushes, difficult paths, and soaking wet feet tested our resolve. Yet, with coffee, a cigarette for Olivier, and renewed determination, we pressed forward to face the final 30 km.

The final stretch was gruelling. Rain poured, the headwind howled, and exhaustion clawed at us. Short supply stops (gels, gels, and more gels!) and DAFCAF kept us going. Finally, seeing the headlights of the car in the dark signaled the end. Crossing the finish line brought euphoria, pride, and the realisation of what we'd achieved. To top it off, Olivier proposed to his girlfriend, creating a moment none of us will forget.

Though fatigue and stiffness soon set in, the pride and joy of completing such a feat overshadowed everything. Thanks to our perfect team, dedicated supporters, generous sponsors, and the tireless crew, it was an unforgettable adventure.

"Let's keep running every f*cking beach in Europe!"

Stage 83

MOITINHA > MELIDES

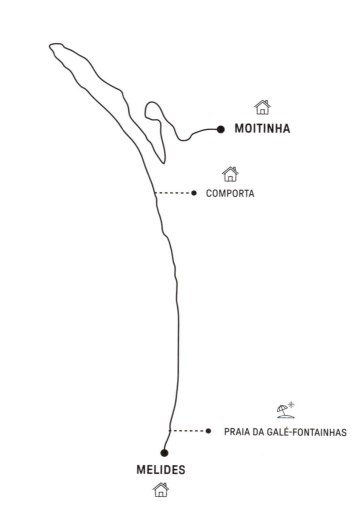

DATE	09/03/2024
DISTANCE	101.74 KM
ELEVATION	561 M
TOTAL TIME	14H38
MOVING TIME	11H34

SHOREHOLDERS
Baptist Gilson
Arnaud Mertens

STAGE HIGHLIGHTS

A journey starting in wetlands, quickly making way for endless sand, tranquil sand beaches.

 Moitinha
The stage begins in this small settlement, setting the tone for a tranquil and scenic journey.

 Comporta
A picturesque village renowned for its stunning beaches, charming atmosphere, and the unique blend of long sandy shores and surrounding rice fields. In summer, it's home to the happy few, with wellness hotels and million-dollar villas rising around the tranquil forests.

 Praia da Galé-Fontainhas
Deserted beach with unique sandy cliff formations far away from the crowd.

 Melides
The stage concludes at this small village near the ocean's edge, a peaceful and scenic endpoint to the journey.

STAGE STORY

We kicked off our adventure a day early with a feast fit for champions: a hearty steak lunch followed by a dinner of fresh fish and rice. It felt more like a culinary tour than preparation for an ultrarun, as if we were more concerned with loading calories than burning them. But the indulgence was short-lived. The next morning, it was game time. Our crew, who had spent the night in the bus, greeted us at the start with 200% energy, their enthusiasm setting the perfect tone for the challenge ahead. With a mix of nerves and excitement, we began our 100 km journey.

The first 30 km were a test of grit as we navigated through rice fields and tall grass on an unforgiving path. The weather seemed to be in a playful mood, throwing everything at us—from blazing sunshine to torrential rain that drenched us completely. The ever-changing scenery and conditions made time feel elastic: some stretches flew by, while others seemed to last forever. PJ's well-timed tips ensured our rest stops were perfectly prepped, each one offering delicious snacks that made it hard to leave.

At one point, during a particularly chaotic downpour, someone jokingly asked, "Got any goggles?" It was the perfect comic relief we needed to keep going. Music wasn't necessary; the real soundtrack was our endless chatter and shared stories. Pro tip for ultrarunners: pick a partner with great tales—and plenty of them.

Our crew's humour and unfiltered encouragement carried us through. Their energy was like stepping into a warm pub on a freezing night—genuine and uplifting. They knew their presence was as vital as our training, turning each gruelling step into something lighter and more enjoyable.

By the 50 km mark, an odd feeling crept in—sadness that the finish line was inching closer. We were having so much fun, laughing and bonding with the crew, that running felt secondary. Along the way, we even set up new Tinder profiles for a laugh, attempting to arrange a date through the organisers. Of course, our mischievous crew swooped in, hijacking the date for themselves and leaving us in fits of laughter.

For me, this was round two of the ultrarun adventure. Instead of quenching my thirst for the experience, it only fuelled my hunger for more. With the memories we made, the crew's camaraderie, and the magic of the journey, one thing is certain: I'll be back for the third edition.

Stage 84

MELIDES > ALMOGRAVE

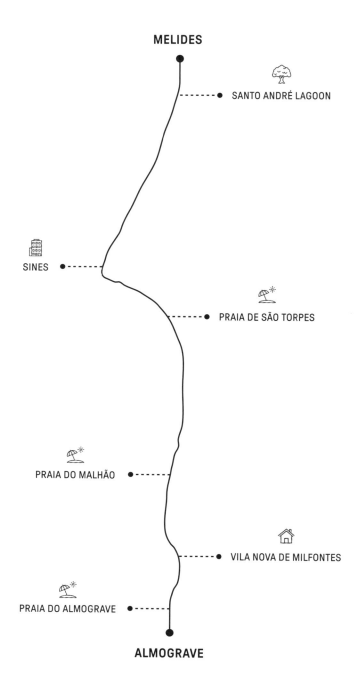

DATE	10/03/2024
DISTANCE	98.3 KM
ELEVATION	1,1170 M
TOTAL TIME	15H10
MOVING TIME	12H36

SHOREHOLDERS
Romy Kint
Nisrien Mortier

STAGE HIGHLIGHTS

Sines
A historic port town with a vibrant maritime history, adding cultural depth to the journey.

Vila Nova de Milfontes
A charming town with a picturesque riverfront and whitewashed buildings, offering a glimpse into traditional Portuguese coastal life.

Santo André Lagoon
A vast wetland area known for its rich birdlife, calm waters, and tranquility.

Praia da São Torpes
A long sandy beach offering excellent surfing conditions.

Praia do Malhão
A wild and rugged beach, untouched by men showcasing raw beauty.

Praia do Almograve
A stunning beach with golden sands and striking cliffs–a breathtaking conclusion to the stage.

STAGE STORY

After days of rain and storms, the weather finally seemed to cooperate for their stage. For Nisrien and Romy, the adventure began with a carefully crafted carboloading plan. They had never eaten so much on purpose, but everything was focused on building energy reserves. The morning of the start was electric with adrenaline. Romy, eager to impress, tried to leap across a river but landed squarely in the water, scattering her gear everywhere. After much laughter and spotting a stunning double rainbow, they were ready to start their long day full of challenges.

The first 30 km felt like a dream: beautiful beaches, little wind, and the ocean showing its strength with spectacular waves. The pace was strong, and at kilometre 25, pancakes provided a welcome boost. But the next stretch brought new challenges—endless sand dunes tested their endurance and forced them to slow down. The realisation of how demanding the day would be began to sink in.

For Nisrien, reaching his first-ever marathon distance was a major milestone, though it came during a mentally draining stretch through the dull streets of Sines. The combination of warm weather and insufficient food during the dunes left him feeling weak and empty. But with a renewed focus on eating, drinking, and caffeine, energy started to return. The landscape after Sines made up for the earlier struggles: a breathtaking coastline with rolling surf and tiny islands. The crew, with their humour and unwavering encouragement, brought bursts of happiness and motivation at every stop.

In Porto Covo, Pauline joined them for the final gruelling kilometres. As darkness fell, every step felt more draining. The lack of light demanded full concentration, and the stunning surroundings disappeared into the night. Romy faced a mental battle, but with Pauline's support and the crew cheering them on, she pushed through.

The last 10 kilometres were pure exhaustion. Both Nisrien and Romy felt their bodies rebelling, but the thought of the finish line kept them moving. When the car lights and music finally appeared in the distance, the relief was overwhelming. They had done it!

After crossing the finish line, the physical pain set in: blisters, sore muscles, and deep cracks from wet feet. But none of it could overshadow the pride and gratitude they felt. Nisrien and Romy had not only overcome the physical challenge but also shared a day filled with emotions, support, and an unbreakable bond.

↱ Regions 9 / 10
Algarve

4,960 km²
467,343 inhabitants

→

PRAIA DOS TRÊS IRMÃOS

GUADIANA INTERNATIONAL BRIDGE, AYAMONTE

↳ The Algarve, Portugal's sun-drenched southern coast, is a mesmerising blend of natural beauty and vibrant tourism. Golden limestone cliffs rise above turquoise waters, framing secluded beaches and hidden coves. While bustling towns like Albufeira and Vilamoura lure sunseekers with lively marinas, championship golf courses, and electric nightlife, the Algarve's essence lies beyond the crowds.

The iconic Benagil sea cave, the pristine islands of Ria Formosa, and Moorish villages like Silves and Tavira offer glimpses into the region's rich heritage. Tavira's Roman bridge and azulejo-clad churches exude old-world charm, while Faro's ancient cobbled streets whisper history.

To the west, Costa Vicentina's cliffs meet the untamed Atlantic, and Cape St. Vincent's fiery sunsets cast an ethereal glow. From cataplana stews to fresh sardines, the Algarve's cuisine is as vibrant as its landscapes—a land of adventure, culture, and serenity where every wave tells a story.

Algarve

155 km Coastline
Capital: Faro

Algarve
↳ Introduction

HOW TO GET THERE

You can reach Algarve best by the airport of Faro, Algarve's capital. Other ways of access are via Seville airport in neighbouring country Spain or through Lisbon airport, the latter demanding likely the most offerings. A 2-3 hour car ride then brings you in Algarve.

WHERE TO STAY

Algarve is a magnet for beach lovers and golf fanatics, featuring no less than 39 golf courses and offers opportunities for everyone from luxury-seeker to party-goer, family to surfer.

Albufeira and Vilamouro offer abundant nightlife with The Strip: Famous for its bars, clubs, and late-night entertainment, attracting party-goers from around the world. Sagres and Praia da Arrifana, on the west Atlantic side, attract surfers, especially in winter times when the waves soar higher. The most luxurious areas of the Algarve are concentrated in the "Golden Triangle", that includes Vilamoura, Quinta do Lago, and Vale do Lobo. Quinta da Lago - known for its exclusive gated communities, luxury villas, and world-class golf courses, Vale do Lobo - famous for its cliffside golf courses, beachfront properties, and a vibrant social scene and Vilamouro - renowned for its glamorous marina lined with yachts, chic boutiques, and fine dining options.

Home to historic towns like Tavira, Lagos, and Silves, the region is rich in Moorish and medieval heritage. The Ria Formosa Natural Park is a haven for birdwatching and eco-tours, while inland areas offer hiking and exploration. Faro, a mid-sized city of 65,000 people, is the administrative capital of the Algarve. It features a historic old town, a vibrant marina, and is close to the Ria Formosa Natural Park. Lagos, Albufeira and Portimao are the other bigger cities in the area.

HISTORY

The Algarve's history is a mixture of influences, shaped by various civilizations over millennia. Early settlements by the Phoenicians, Carthaginians, and Romans left a legacy of trade, agriculture, and infrastructure, such as bridges and aqueducts.

The most profound influence came from the Moors, who ruled from the 8th to the 13th century and named the region "Al-Gharb" (The West). Their legacy is seen in the region's architecture, with whitewashed houses and distinctive chimneys, irrigation systems, and the introduction of crops like almonds and citrus. Cities like Silves, once the Moorish capital, still showcase their influence through its castle and ancient walls. The Reconquista in the 13th century brought the Algarve under Portuguese rule, but it retained its unique Moorish character. In the 15th and 16th centuries, the region became a hub for Portugal's Age of Discoveries, with Lagos serving as a major port for explorers and traders. Figures like Prince Henry the Navigator made the Algarve a centre for maritime innovation, launching voyages that expanded global trade.

The 1755 Lisbon earthquake also devastated the Algarve, destroying many historic structures, but the region rebuilt, blending its ancient charm with new influences. Today, visitors can explore medieval castles, Roman ruins, and Moorish fortifications that tell the Algarve's rich story.

In recent decades, the Algarve has experienced a surge in tourism, becoming one of Europe's most sought-after destinations. Known for its stunning beaches, luxury resorts, and year-round mild climate, the region now draws millions of visitors annually. The tourism boom has brought development, with areas like Vilamoura, Albufeira, and Lagos offering a mix of nightlife, golf courses, and family-friendly activities. Despite this, the Algarve has managed to preserve much of its natural and cultural heritage, with protected areas like the Ria Formosa Natural Park and traditional villages maintaining their authentic charm. This blend of history and modernity makes the Algarve a unique destination.

ALGARVE

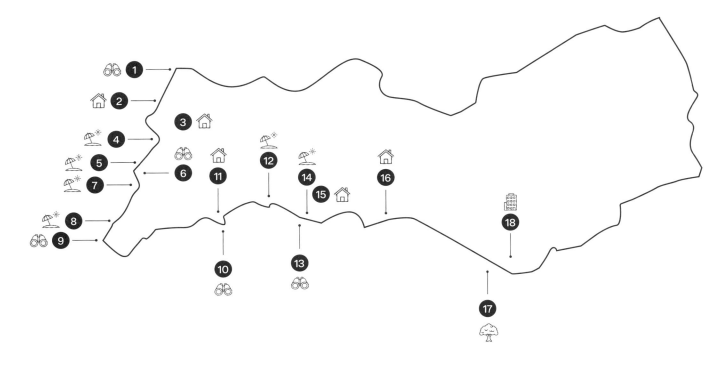

PORTUGAL

EXPLORE / HIGHLIGHTS

1. Cabo Sardão
2. Praia de Odeceixe
3. Aljezur
4. Praia da Arrifana
5. Praia da Bordeira
6. Pontal da Carrapateira
7. Praia do Amado
8. Praia do Castelejo
9. Cabo de São Vincent & Sagres
10. Ponta da Piedade
11. Lagos
12. Praia da Rocha
13. Benagil Cave
14. Praia da Marinha
15. Lagoa & Porches
16. Albufeira
17. Ria Formosa Natural Park
18. Faro

REGION 9 / 10

FORTALEZA DE SAGRES

Algarve
↳ Highlights

The Algarve region, often celebrated as Portugal's sunlit jewel, is a stunning fusion of golden beaches, dramatic cliffs, and vibrant culture. Stretching along the southern coast, it is adorned with picturesque fishing villages, azure waters, and hidden coves.

Faro, the region's historic capital, enchants with its cobbled streets, ancient walls and lively marina, while destinations like Lagos and Albufeira offer a mix of natural beauty and lively nightlife. The Algarve is famed for its fresh seafood, world-class golf courses, and awe-inspiring sea caves such as those at Benagil. It's a haven for sun-seekers, adventurers, and those looking to immerse themselves in Portugal's coastal charm.

1. CABO SARDÃO

This remote cape is famous for its dramatic cliffs and spectacular views of the Atlantic. It's also a key spot for birdwatching, including white storks that nest on the cliffs – a rare phenomenon worldwide.

2. PRAIA DE ODECEIXE

A picturesque village marking the border of Alentejo and Algarve, Praia de Odeceixe is unique, with a river that creates calm swimming spots on one side and surf-friendly ocean waves on the other. The surrounding cliffs provide spectacular hiking opportunities.

3. ALJEZUR

Aljezur is a historic town with whitewashed houses, a Moorish castle, and a peaceful vibe. Nearby Praia da Amoreira is known for its blend of ocean and river landscapes, perfect for surfing, paddleboarding, or simply admiring the beauty of the dunes and estuary.

4. PRAIA DA ARRIFANA

This surfing hotspot and quaint village is backed by dramatic cliffs. Its crescent-shaped bay offers a sheltered spot for surfers of all levels. Enjoy breathtaking cliff views from the ruins of an ancient fortress nearby.

5. PRAIA DA BORDEIRA

The village of Carrapateira is a gateway to some of the Algarve's wildest beaches. Praia da Bordeira features vast sands and dunes, while wooden boardwalks offer panoramic views of the dramatic coastline. A must-visit for surfers and nature enthusiasts alike.

6. PONTAL DA CARRAPATEIRA

This scenic viewpoint offers breathtaking vistas of the dramatic coastline. Wooden boardwalks make it easy to explore while taking in the panoramic views of towering cliffs, rolling waves, and sandy beaches below. A must-visit spot for photographers and hikers.

7. PRAIA DO AMADO

A surfer's paradise with consistent waves and a stunning backdrop of rugged cliffs, it's a favourite for surf schools and competitions, but also offers tranquillity for beachgoers. Surrounded by natural beauty, it's ideal for those seeking adventure and serenity alike.

8. PRAIA DO CASTELEJO & DA CORDOAMA

These neighbouring beaches near Vila do Bispo are known for their wild, untouched beauty. Towering cliffs, soft sands, and powerful waves make them ideal for surfers, photographers, and sunset seekers.

9. CABO DE SÃO VINCENT & SAGRES

The southwesternmost point of Europe, Cape St. Vincent is a place of maritime and historical significance. Known as the "End of the World," it features the Sagres Fortress, linked to Prince Henry the Navigator. Rebuilt in the 16th century, it was central to Portugal's Age of Discoveries. Nearby, the iconic lighthouse guiding ships along the dramatic cliffs dates back to 1846 and is one of the most powerful in Europe.

SALT FIELD IN OLHÃO

The town of Sagres, close by, gave its name to the popular Sagres beer, a symbol of the region's adventurous spirit. Visitors often enjoy breathtaking views and a refreshing Sagres to conclude their visit.

10. PONTA DA PIEDADE

Just south of Lagos is a stunning coastal area renowned for its golden rock formations, dramatic cliffs and crystal-clear waters. Explore by boat, kayak, or on foot for unforgettable views and sunsets.

11. LAGOS

This tourist hotspot offers a charming mix of cobblestone streets, historic churches and vibrant nightlife. Visit the Igreja de Santo António, and explore its rich maritime history.

12. PRAIA DA ROCHA

Praia da Rocha is one of the Algarve's most iconic beaches, with expansive golden sands and vibrant surroundings. Enjoy water sports, beach bars and a lively promenade. The nearby Fortaleza de Santa Catarina offers historic charm and stunning views of the coastline.

13. BENAGIL CAVE

This stunning sea cave with a natural skylight, golden cliffs and turquoise waters, is now accessible only via guided tours. Swimming or disembarking is prohibited, preserving its beauty and ensuring safety. Explore by boat or kayak with certified guides!

14. PRAIA DA MARINHA

One of Europe's most beautiful beaches, with crystal-clear waters and iconic cliffs. A perfect spot for swimming, snorkelling, or admiring the postcard-worthy scenery.

15. LAGOA & PORCHES

Explore Lagoa's quaint old town and nearby Porches, known for its traditional pottery. Visit the pottery workshops or the 18th-century Chapel of Nossa Senhora da Rocha, perched on a cliff with panoramic sea views.

16. ALBUFEIRA

A lively beach town with golden sands and vibrant nightlife. Ideal for families, water sports enthusiasts, or anyone seeking fun by the sea.

17. RIA FORMOSA NATURAL PARK

Just to the south of Faro is this lagoon system of wetlands and islands, perfect for birdwatching, hiking, and boat tours. Discover its unique biodiversity and scenic tranquillity. Ilha Deserta offers untouched beaches, while Ilha da Culatra is a fishing community with a laid-back atmosphere and fresh seafood.

18. FARO

The Algarve's capital blends history, culture and nature. Its charming old town, encircled by ancient walls, features cobblestone streets, the Arco da Vila town gate, and the stunning Cathedral of Faro. With lively markets, vibrant cafés, and its role as a gateway to idyllic islands like Ilha Deserta, Faro is a must-visit gem.

↰ PARQUE NATURAL DO SUDOESTE ALENTEJANO E COSTA VICENTINA

ALJEZUR ↳

ALJEZUR

FARO DE CABO SARDAO, CAVALEIRO

↰ TAVIRA SALT FIELDS

FÁBRICA, VILA NOVA DE CACELA ↳

↰ PRAIA DE FÁBRICA, VILA NOVA DE CACELA

OLHÃO ↴

Stage 85

ALMOGRAVE > PRAIA DO AMADO

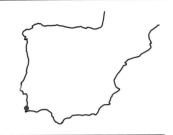

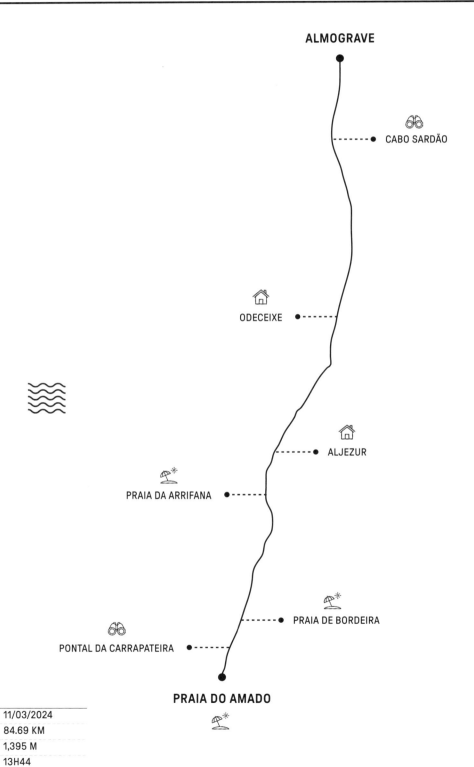

DATE	11/03/2024
DISTANCE	84.69 KM
ELEVATION	1,395 M
TOTAL TIME	13H44
MOVING TIME	10H50

SHOREHOLDERS
Arthur Chambre
Amélie Harvengt

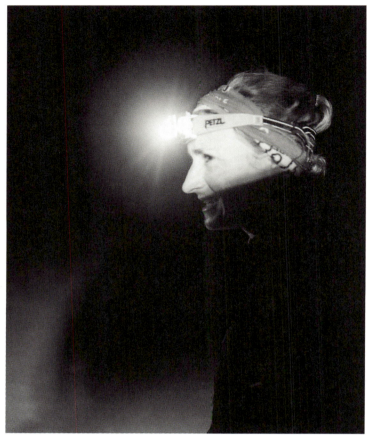

STAGE HIGHLIGHTS

 Odeceixe
A quaint village known for its idyllic river beach and whitewashed houses on rolling hills. Praia de Odeceixe blends river and sea in perfect harmony.

 Aljezur
A historic town featuring a 10th-century Moorish castle with sweeping valley views, adding cultural depth to the journey.

 Praia da Arrifana
A crescent-shaped bay surrounded by steep cliffs, attracting surfers and nature lovers

 Praia de Bordeira
A vast expanse of golden sand and dunes.

 Pontal de Carrapateira
Dramatic cliffs and coastal trails offering breathtaking views of the Algarve.

 Praia do Amado
A surfers' paradise framed by rugged cliffs, embodying wild and adventure.

 Cabo Sardão
A dramatic cliffside cape offering panoramic views of the Atlantic, with towering rock formations.

STAGE STORY

We chose this stage crossing the Southwest Alentejo and Vicentine Coast Natural Park because we primarily wanted a route focused on trail running while enjoying landscapes that promised to be spectacular.

From the very first kilometres, the scenery did not disappoint: the coastline revealed itself in its wildest and most unspoiled form, offering breathtaking panoramas. From the top of the cliffs, we constantly overlooked the ocean, rewarding us with absolutely stunning views. However, such beauty came at a price: the route was demanding, with significant elevation gain. Every time water had carved its way from land to sea, we had to navigate particularly technical sections, sometimes close to climbing. But these few hundred meters of intense effort allowed us to avoid detours of up to 5km.

Beyond the rugged terrain, the nature of the ground also complicated our progress: the omnipresent sand significantly slowed our pace. By 5 pm, after ten hours of running, we had covered only half of our planned route—50 kilometres out of the 100 initially envisioned. Knowing that we had only an hour and a half before sunset, we made the prudent decision to modify our itinerary. Following the cliffs at night would have been far too dangerous—the trails were numerous and already difficult to navigate in daylight. We therefore opted for a safer route, taking larger paths to reach our destination. We then continued along a long gravel track, a much faster surface than sand, allowing us to pick up speed. From the 60th kilometre, Amélie and I naturally increased our pace, leading Damien to stop at the 70th Kilometre. As night fell, we switched on our headlamps before reaching the seashore, where the trail had less elevation and offered better running conditions.

It was then that we crossed Praia de Bordeira, a vast beach enveloped in such dense fog that our visibility was reduced to barely five meters. Deprived of landmarks in this almost surreal atmosphere, we moved forward blindly, immersed in an ambiance as mysterious as it was mesmerizing. After a long moment of uncertainty, a small light finally appeared in the distance—it was Max, who had come to guide us through this tricky section. Only about ten kilometres remained. Carried by the excitement of the approaching finish, we pressed on with renewed energy. Finally, after 85 kilometres of effort, we reached Praia do Amado.

While we felt great satisfaction in completing this stage, a slight disappointment remained—we had not reached the hoped-for 100 kilometres. But this is only a postponement: Spain will undoubtedly offer us a new opportunity to take on this challenge in an upcoming stage.

Stage 86

PRAIA DO AMADO > PRAIA DA ROCHA

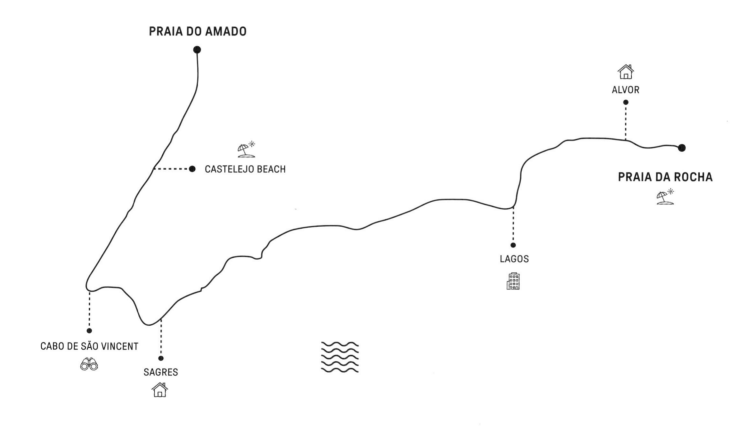

DATE	12/03/2024
DISTANCE	104 KM
ELEVATION	1,172 M
TOTAL TIME	12H05
MOVING TIME	11H15

SHOREHOLDER
Hugo Oliveira

PRAIA DOS TRÊS IRMÃOS

STAGE HIGHLIGHTS

 Sagres
A town rich in maritime heritage, home to the imposing Sagres Fortress and a laid-back vibe cherished by surfers and adventurers.

 Lagos
A lively town where history meets natural splendour. Highlights are Ponta da Piedade's golden cliffs and Praia Dona Ana's crystal-clear waters and striking rock formations.

 Alvor
A charming village offering a quieter retreat with boardwalks, sandy beaches, and traditional Portuguese charm.

 Praia da Rocha
A vibrant hub in Portimão, known for its wide beach, lively nightlife, and breathtaking cliff views.

 Castelejo Beach
Nestled amidst towering cliffs, this serene spot is known for its rugged beauty and powerful surf, setting a dramatic tone for the stage.

 Cabo de São Vincent
Europe's southwesternmost point, featuring Europe's dramatic southernmost point.

STAGE STORY

My name is Hugo Oliveira, a 37-year-old athlete with Brazilian roots. Let me share a truly memorable story about how a coincidental encounter with Max led to an adventure of a lifetime. I've spent the last nine years living in the beautiful southern region of Portugal, in Aljezur, Algarve. Sport has always been my anchor, deeply ingrained in my life from childhood. For the past 25 years, running has been my constant companion, offering me solace and clarity. The allure of testing my limits has always driven me, pushing past barriers to achieve more.

One day, while managing a guesthouse in Algarve, I met Max—a meeting that would change everything. Max noticed my Hoka running t-shirt. That sparked a conversation about running, and he shared details about his project Follow the Coast, about runners taking on a unique multi-stage, 100 km endurance challenge.

Max explained that the event was designed to test runners, with 24-hour time limits for each 100 km stage. Hearing about this, I thought, "What an amazing challenge!" Max then left for a coffee break, returning with unexpected news—two participants had dropped out of Stage 86, and he offered me the opportunity to take their place. Without hesitation, I responded, "When? Tomorrow?" Surprised by my eagerness, Max smiled as I added, "When life presents an opportunity, seize it!"

The next day, I found myself preparing for the challenge, gathering gels and supplements despite having recently completed an Ironman race. Still, the excitement of running 100km along the Algarve's stunning coastline was irresistible.

The journey was incredible—a route filled with dramatic cliffs, hidden beaches, and a staggering 1,500 m of elevation gain. Each step brought me closer to nature's raw beauty, immersing me in the rugged charm of the Algarve. I remembered friends who had suggested exploring the coast on foot, but I had always replied, "If I do it, it'll be by running." And now, here I was, fulfilling that promise.

This challenge tested every ounce of my mental and physical strength. But as I crossed the finish line, I felt an overwhelming sense of accomplishment and gratitude. Follow the Coast had given me an unforgettable experience—a chance to push my boundaries and create memories that will last a lifetime.

Sometimes, life's most extraordinary adventures begin with a simple yes.

Stage 87

PRAIA DA ROCHA > OLHÃO

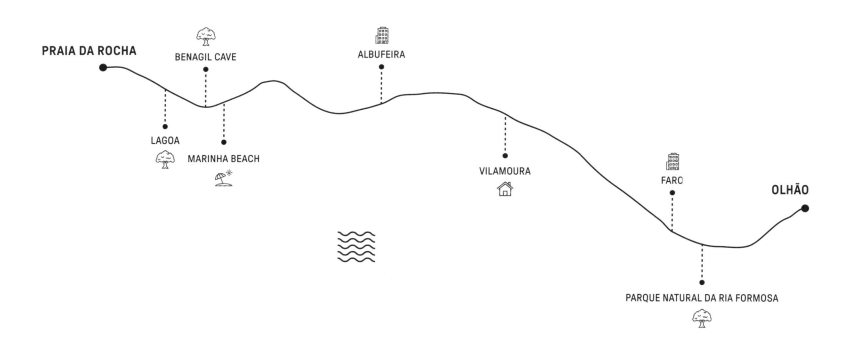

DATE	13/03/2024
DISTANCE	100.1 KM
ELEVATION	1,161 M
TOTAL TIME	15H12
MOVING TIME	13H32

SHOREHOLDERS
Richard Kruijskamp
Viktor Huegen

STAGE HIGHLIGHTS

 Albufeira
A bustling town blending traditional charm with energetic nightlife.

 Vilamoura
Famous for its luxurious marina, world-class golf courses, and upscale vibe.

 Faro
The historic capital of the Algarve, featuring cobbled streets and ancient walls.

 Lagoa
A charming area with serene countryside and vineyards, offering a peaceful contrast to the coastal energy.

 Benagil Cave
A natural wonder with a dome-shaped interior illuminated by a skylight.

 Marinha Beach
Renowned for its cliffs and clear waters, ranked among Europe's most beautiful beaches.

 Parque Natural da Ria Formosa
A unique coastal lagoon teeming with wildlife, providing a serene transition to the journey's end.

STAGE STORY

When co-founder Max introduced Richard to the Follow the Coast project in July 2023, it sparked an idea that quickly took root. By the time Max mentioned an open spot in Stage 87, Richard didn't hesitate to say yes—and his friend Viktor was just as easily convinced. Neither had ever run an ultra-distance race, let alone a gruelling 100 km stretch along the hilly Algarve coast. But they were inspired and decided to dedicate their effort to a higher purpose: supporting the War Child Foundation. Their mission was not only personal but also about raising awareness for children affected by war, advocating for a safer future.

Fall and winter 2023 were spent training in the Netherlands, battling rain and wind through the national parks. Despite minor injuries, their motivation never wavered. On March 10, they stood ready to carve their path into running history.

Their journey began in Portimão, where the industrial port quickly gave way to the Algarve's stunning cliffs, caves, and beaches. However, beauty came with a price—steep ascents, rocky descents, and slippery trails defined the next 40 km. Though the pace slowed, the duo made the most of their surroundings, marvelling at the coastline while laughing at how much they'd underestimated the challenge, especially the altitude gain. By late morning, the sun began to heat up—a stark contrast to their cold, rainy training in the Netherlands. Cooling breezes and the occasional ice-cold drink from the crew kept them moving.

Midway through the stage, they reached Albufeira, bustling with tourists enjoying leisurely lunches. As they passed, a waiter joked about their unusual appearance—clearly not your typical tourists.

Dusk fell as they approached the Ria Formosa Natural Park near Faro. Wooden boardwalks replaced the rocky terrain, offering stunning views of the park's tranquil beauty. After crossing the Faro airport, they entered the city centre, where their crew welcomed them with plant-based burgers. Fuelled by the brief respite (perhaps too eagerly consumed), they pushed into the final stretch.

The last few kilometres tested their endurance to the limit. Running along a highway in darkness, with techno beats blasting from the support van, they leaned on each other to push through. Exhausted but triumphant, they crossed the finish line. It was a journey filled with struggle, camaraderie, and unforgettable memories—proving that even in the toughest challenges, the spirit of adventure prevails.

Stage 88

OLHÃO > ISLA CANELA

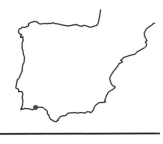

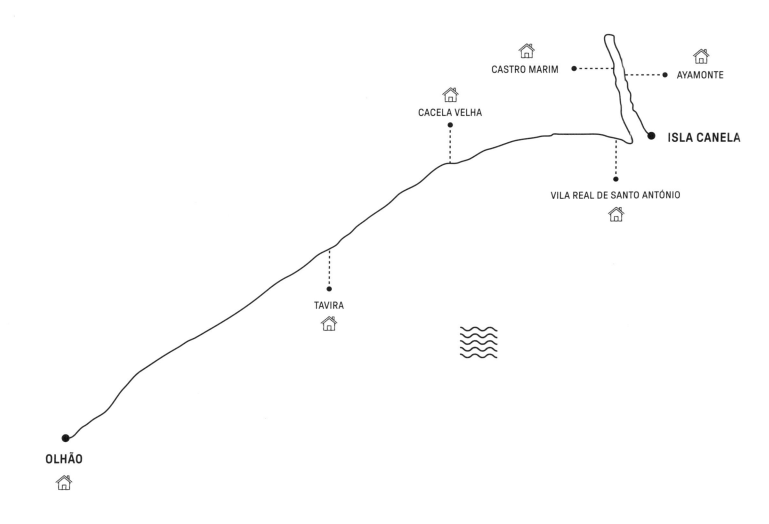

DATE	14/03/2024
DISTANCE	100.15 KM
ELEVATION	303 M
TOTAL TIME	13H31
MOVING TIME	12H12

SHOREHOLDER
Adam Wade

STAGE HIGHLIGHTS

Olhão
The stage begins in this charming town, celebrated for its seafood and proximity to the stunning Parque Natural da Ria Formosa.

Cacela Velha
A picturesque village with whitewashed houses and an ancient fort.

Tavira
A highlight of the stage, known for its cobbled streets, historic churches, and the iconic Roman-era Tavira Old Bridge over the Gilão River.

Castro Marim
A touch of medieval charm with its hilltop castle.

Vila Real de Santo António
A town with elegant Pombaline architecture set along the Guadiana River.

Ayamonte
Crossing the Guadiana International Bridge, runners enter Spain and arrive in this vibrant riverside town with a lively atmosphere.

STAGE STORY

What an honour to to do another Follow The Coast stage and contribute once again to this epic story written 100 km at a time! This time, I had the incredible support of my dear wife, Lindsay, who has her own running goals after completing her first marathon this year—next stop, an Follow the Coast stage, hopefully! As always, a huge shoutout goes to the legend Max, whose unwavering support, day in and day out, lifts every runner to new heights. From his words of encouragement to blasting Jimi Hendrix, Prodigy, and dance classics from the van, Max's energy pulled me through those gruelling final kilometres.

This stage was special because it marked the end of Portugal and the start of Spain. The landscape couldn't have been more different from Stage 21, which I had tackled previously. Gone were the rugged cliffs and steep ascents. Instead, this route was astonishingly flat—a welcome change in some ways, but deceptively tough due to over 20 km of relentless beach running. The soft sand was unforgiving, draining energy with every step and making the long stretches feel endless.

Starting in Olhão, the stage took me through the idyllic eastern Algarve, past Tavira with its historic charm and the iconic Old Bridge. Running through Cacela Velha, I soaked in views of the pristine coastline before heading into Vila Real de Santo António, a town steeped in maritime history. Castro Marim, with its ancient castle, added a medieval touch before the journey brought me to the Guadiana International Bridge. Crossing into Spain felt monumental—a symbolic moment as well as a physical transition.

The final stretch led to Ayamonte, with its charming riverside vibes, and then onto Isla Canela, where I was greeted by its expansive beaches. The finish line marked not just the end of this stage but also the continuation of a journey that feels bigger than any single run.

As I reflect on this incredible experience, I'll end as I did after my first stage: "This was the second stage I did, and it will definitely not be the last…"

Regions 10 / 10
Andalusia

87,597 km²
8.6 million inhabitants

10

→ PLAYA DE CANELA, ISLA CANELA

MARISMAS DE SAN MIGUEL

↳ Andalusia, Spain's largest and most diverse region, stretches from the fertile Guadalquivir Valley to the sparkling Mediterranean and Atlantic coastlines.

Its endless beaches, kissed by sunlight, invite relaxation and adventure. The region's Moorish heritage thrives in Seville and Granada, with intricate palaces and lush gardens.

Andalusia's wetlands teem with life, from storks and flamingos to vast rice fields, sustaining both traditions and wildlife. Dotted along the hills, whitewashed villages like Vejer de la Frontera offer both a glimpse into a rich past, and breathtaking vistas.

The coastline is a paradise for surfers and kitesurfers, with Tarifa renowned for its strong winds and vibrant scene. Nearby, the iconic Rock of Gibraltar marks the meeting point of Europe and Africa. Andalusia is renowned for its olive groves, horses, and cuisine featuring gazpacho, jamón ibérico, and sherry. Whether exploring its ancient cities or relaxing on shores, Andalusia offers an unforgettable journey into the soul of Spain.

Andalusia

1,000 km Coastline
Capital: Seville

Andalusia
↳ Introduction

HOW TO GET THERE

Andalusia, Spain's largest and most diverse region, is well-connected and easy to explore. Major airports like Málaga (AGP), Seville (SVQ), and Granada (GRX) serve international and domestic travellers, with Málaga offering the best access to the Costa del Sol. For those travelling within Spain, high-speed AVE trains link Seville, Córdoba, and Málaga to Madrid and Barcelona, making arrival fast and scenic.

Once in Andalusia, getting around depends on your itinerary. The high-speed and regional trains are ideal for connecting major cities, while an extensive bus network links smaller towns and rural areas. For ultimate flexibility, renting a car is the best way to explore whitewashed villages, natural parks, and coastal gems like Tarifa. In cities like Seville or Málaga, bikes and walking are perfect for discovering historic centres, while rural areas are best explored by car.

This combination of transport options ensures you can enjoy both Andalusia's cultural hubs and hidden gems, from bustling cities to serene beaches.

WHERE TO STAY

Andalusia offers something for everyone. For surfers, Tarifa is a top choice with its strong winds and laid-back vibe, while Caños de Meca provides quieter surf-friendly spots. Hikers will enjoy Grazalema or Ronda, ideal for exploring the Sierra de Grazalema, or coastal trails near Los Alcornocales Natural Park. Families will find Málaga perfect with its beaches, museums, and nearby attractions like Nerja and the Costa del Sol.

For nightlife, Marbella and Puerto Banús are the hubs of luxury and lively bars. Culture enthusiasts should explore Seville, Granada, or Córdoba, where history comes alive in the cathedrals, palaces, and historic quarters. For a blend of experiences, Cádiz combines sandy beaches, vibrant nightlife, and rich history, while white villages like Vejer de la Frontera or Arcos de la Frontera offer peace, charm, and stunning landscapes. Andalusia promises the perfect base for any traveller.

HISTORY

Andalusia's history is a captivating tapestry shaped by diverse cultures over millennia. Its story begins with prehistoric cave dwellers, evident in sites like the Cueva de la Pileta, and evolves with the arrival of ancient civilisations. The Phoenicians established coastal trading hubs like Cádiz, while the Romans left a legacy of cities such as Itálica, showcasing amphitheaters and aqueducts.

The most transformative period began in 711 AD with the arrival of the Moors, who ruled for nearly eight centuries. Andalusia flourished as a centre of art, science, and architecture under the Moors, leaving behind masterpieces like the Alhambra in Granada, the Mezquita of Córdoba, and Seville's Giralda. This era also saw the blending of Muslim, Christian, and Jewish traditions, creating a unique cultural identity.

In 1492, the Reconquista brought Andalusia under Catholic rule, marking the end of Moorish dominance. That same year, Christopher Columbus set sail from Huelva, ushering in Spain's Age of Exploration. The region's ports, particularly Seville, became global trade hubs, enriching its cities and shaping its character. Today, Andalusia's rich history is alive in its architecture, festivals, and traditions, making it a region of timeless allure and cultural depth.

ANDALUSIA

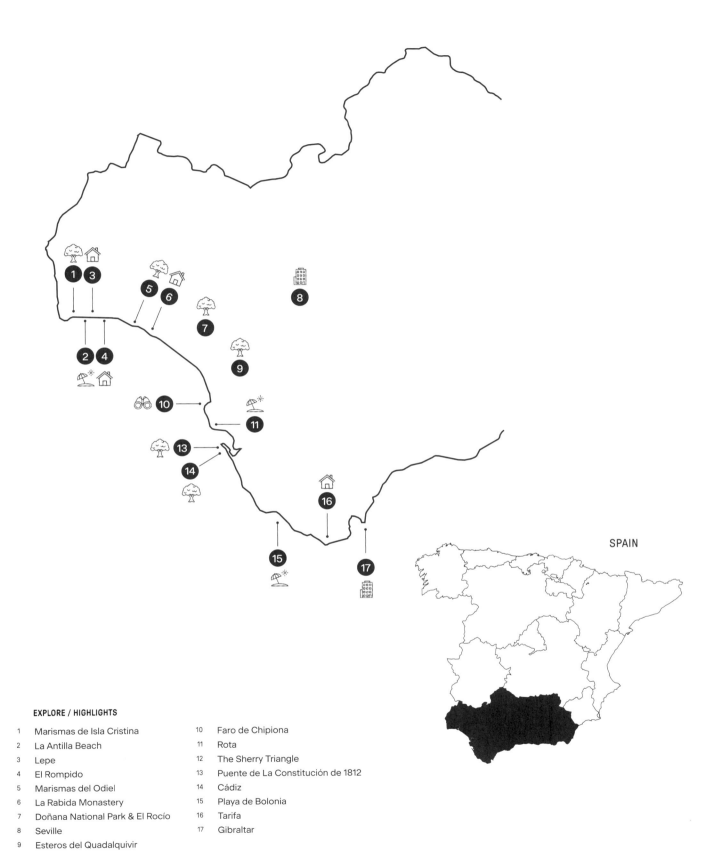

EXPLORE / HIGHLIGHTS

1. Marismas de Isla Cristina
2. La Antilla Beach
3. Lepe
4. El Rompido
5. Marismas del Odiel
6. La Rabida Monastery
7. Doñana National Park & El Rocío
8. Seville
9. Esteros del Quadalquivir
10. Faro de Chipiona
11. Rota
12. The Sherry Triangle
13. Puente de La Constitución de 1812
14. Cádiz
15. Playa de Bolonia
16. Tarifa
17. Gibraltar

Andalusia
↳ Highlights

Andalusia, often hailed as Spain's vibrant southern heart, is a captivating blend of sun-soaked beaches, historic treasures, and rich cultural heritage. Spanning from the Mediterranean coastline to the rugged Sierra Nevada mountains, this region enchants with its Moorish architecture, flamenco rhythms, and stunning landscapes.

Seville, the region's spirited capital, dazzles with its iconic cathedral, Alcázar palace, and lively tapas bars, while cities like Granada and Córdoba boast architectural marvels such as the Alhambra and the Mezquita. Along the Costa del Sol, destinations like Málaga and Marbella beckon with golden sands, azure waters, and a cosmopolitan vibe.

1. MARISMAS DE ISLA CRISTINA

This protected area of wetlands and salt flats is a must-see for nature lovers. It offers walking and cycling trails through a unique ecosystem of tidal marshes. It's ideal for spotting diverse bird species, especially during migration.

2. LA ANTILLA BEACH

La Antilla Beach is a favourite for locals and visitors alike. Its fine sand and calm waters make it perfect for families. Lined with chiringuitos (beach bars), it offers fresh seafood and a lively atmosphere. Walk along the promenade at sunset or try paddleboarding for a fun, active experience.

3. LEPE

Lepe is more than its beaches—it has a rich cultural side. Visit the historic San Cristóbal Church, known for its unique tower, and explore the town's local crafts and gastronomy. The Museum of Marine Salt showcases traditional salt production methods.

4. EL ROMPIDO

El Rompido is a quaint fishing village with colourful boats and a relaxed atmosphere. Wander through its charming streets, dine on fresh seafood, and enjoy views of the Río Piedras. The twin lighthouses—one historic, one modern—are must-sees. From here, take a ferry to the pristine Flecha del Rompido, a sandbank with tranquil beaches ideal for swimming or nature walks.

5. MARISMAS DEL ODIEL

This UNESCO Biosphere Reserve is a haven for birdwatchers and nature enthusiasts. The tidal wetlands are home to flamingos, spoonbills, and other species. Explore its diverse habitats via walking trails or guided tours. The observation towers provide stunning panoramas of the marshes and the opportunity to spot wildlife in its natural environment.

6. LA RÁBIDA MONUSTERY & MONUMENTO DE COLON

A historic gem, La Rábida Monastery is where Christopher Columbus prepared for his voyage to the New World. The 14th-century Franciscan monastery features beautifully preserved cloisters and a museum with artifacts from Columbus's time.

7. DOÑANA NATIONAL PARK

Doñana National Park is a UNESCO World Heritage Site and one of Europe's most important wetlands. Spanning over 100,000 hectares, it boasts a stunning mosaic of ecosystems, including marshes, dunes, pine forests, and lagoons. It's home to rare species like the Iberian lynx and Spanish imperial eagle, as well as countless migratory birds. Visitors can explore its beauty via guided 4x4 tours, hiking trails, or riverboats along the Guadalquivir.

8. SEVILLE

Seville, the vibrant capital of Andalusia, is a city of history, culture, and flamenco spirit. Iconic landmarks include the majestic Seville Cathedral, the world's largest Gothic cathedral, and the Giralda Tower, offering breathtaking views. The Alcázar of Seville, a UNESCO site, showcases exquisite Mudéjar architecture. Stroll through the lively Santa Cruz neighbourhood, with its narrow streets and charming squares, or relax in the lush Maria Luisa

ESTEROS DEL QUADALQUIVIR

ROCK OF GIBRALTAR

Park. Don't miss the Plaza de España, a stunning blend of history and modernity. Rich in festivals, tapas, and tradition, Seville captivates all who visit.

9. ESTEROS DEL QUADALQUIVIR

The Esteros del Guadalquivir are a network of saltwater marshes and estuaries near the mouth of the Guadalquivir River. These wetlands are vital for biodiversity, serving as a sanctuary for migratory birds like flamingos, and herons. Visitors can explore the region through guided tours or self-led walks, immersing themselves in the landscape's serene beauty.

10. FARO DE CHIPIONA

The Chipiona Lighthouse, at 69 m Spain's tallest, offers breathtaking views of the coast and the Guadalquivir estuary. Climb its 344 steps for a panoramic perspective. Nearby, the beaches of Chipiona, such as Playa de Regla, are ideal for swimming and sunbathing. Don't miss the charming old town with its vibrant market and traditional Andalusian atmosphere.

11. ROTA

Rota's beaches, like Playa de la Costilla, offer golden sands and crystal-clear waters. Explore the historic Castillo de Luna, a medieval fortress, or the lively Mercado Central for local delicacies. Rota's rich naval history and vibrant culinary scene, featuring fresh seafood and local wines, make it a memorable stop.

12. THE SHERRY TRIANGLE

Formed by three towns – Jerez de la Frontera, Sanlúcar de Barrameda and El Puerto de Santa María – the Sherry Triangle is famous for its jerez, a fortified wine with a rich history and unique flavours.

13. PUENTE DE LA CONSTITUCIÓN DE 1812

The Puente de la Constitución de 1812, also known as La Pepa Bridge, is an iconic structure in Cádiz and one of Spain's longest bridges. Opened in 2015, it spans 3,092 meters across the Bay of Cádiz, connecting the city with Puerto Real.

14. CADIZ

Cádiz, one of Europe's oldest cities, is a captivating blend of history, culture, and seaside charm. Its old town is a labyrinth of narrow streets leading to iconic landmarks like the Cádiz Cathedral with its golden dome and the Tavira Tower, offering panoramic views. Relax along the picturesque La Caleta Beach or stroll the lively Plaza de las Flores. The city's vibrant Mercado Central showcases fresh seafood and local flavours. Don't miss the Carnival of Cádiz, one of Spain's most famous festivals.

15. VEJER DE LA FRONTERA

Vejer de la Frontera is a whitewashed hilltop town with Moorish influences, known for its winding streets, flower-filled courtyards, and panoramic viewpoints. Plaza de España serves as a lively gathering spot, while local markets offer handmade crafts and Andalusian cuisine.

16. PLAYA DE BOLONIA

Playa de Bolonia is a stunning beach near Tarifa, known for its clear waters and the majestic Duna de Bolonia, a massive sand dune. It's also home to Baelo Claudia, a well-preserved Roman city with ruins of a forum, theater, and fish salting factories.

17. TARIFA

Tarifa, Europe's southernmost town, is a haven for windsurfing and kitesurfing thanks to its strong winds and stunning beaches. The historic Castle of Guzmán el Bueno, overlooking the Strait of Gibraltar, offers incredible views of Africa. The charming old town's narrow streets are lined with cafes and boutiques.

18. GIBRALTAR

Gibraltar, a British Overseas Territory since 1713, sits at the southern tip of Spain. The iconic Rock of Gibraltar, standing at 426 meters, dominates the landscape and offers breathtaking views of Europe and Africa. Visitors can hike to the summit via trails like the Mediterranean Steps or take a cable car for convenience.

↰ PLAYA DE SAN MIGUEL, RIO PIEDRAS

MONUMENTO A COLON, HUELVA ↳

MUELLE DE RIOTINTO, HUELVA

PLAYA DE NUEVA UMBRIA

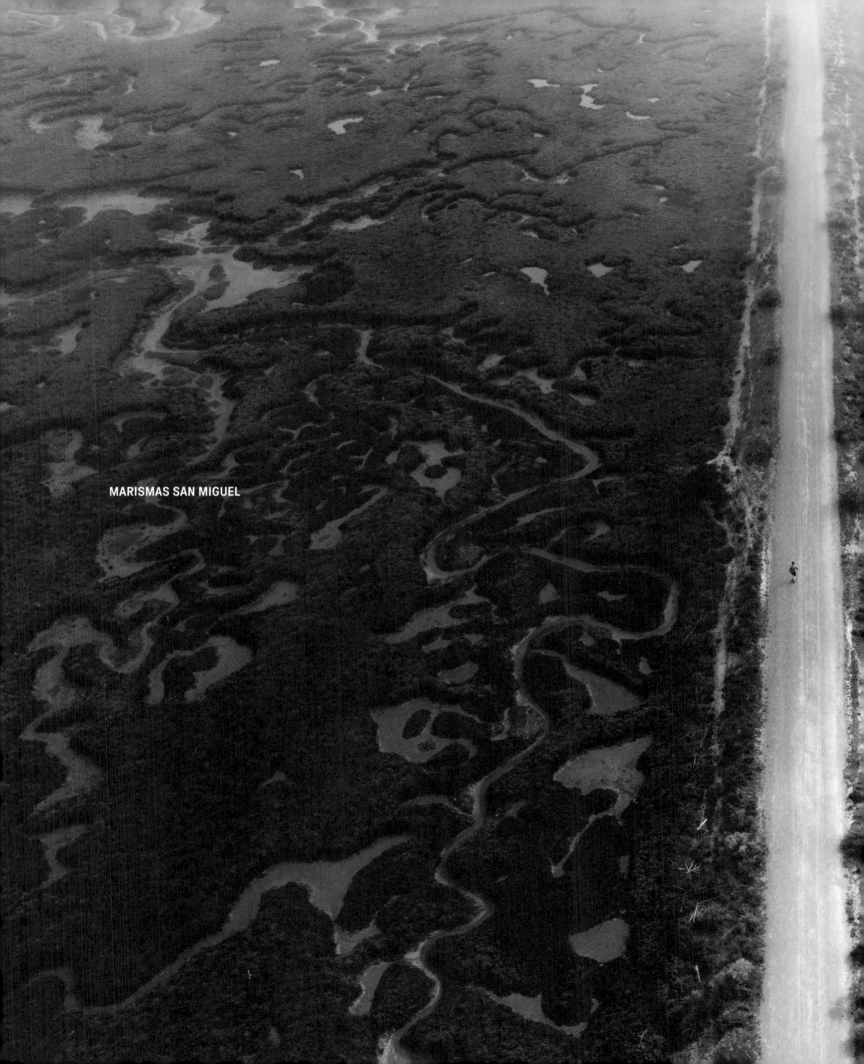
MARISMAS SAN MIGUEL

↰ CHIPIONA　　　　　　　　　　　　　　　　　　　　　　　　ESTEROS DEL GUADALQUIVIR ↳

↰ ESTEROS DEL GUADALQUIVIR

CHIPIONA LIGTHOUSE, CHIPIONA ↴

Stage 89

ISLA CANELA > LEPE

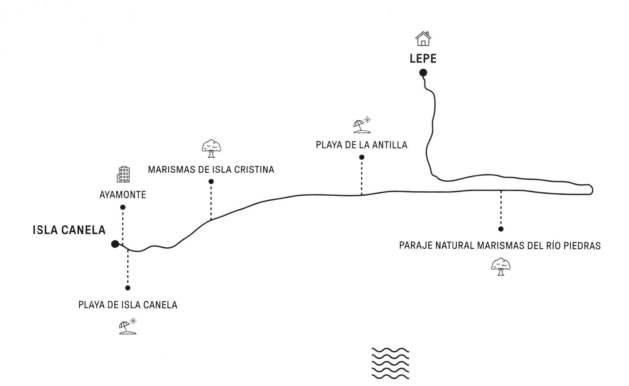

DATE	15/03/2024
DISTANCE	100.29 KM
ELEVATION	856 M
TOTAL TIME	14H01
MOVING TIME	13H56

SHOREHOLDER
Simon Corne

STAGE HIGHLIGHTS

 Ayamonte
The stage begins in this historic town, known for its whitewashed houses, charming streets, and stunning views of the Guadiana River.

 Lepe
A charming town where Andalusian traditions meet the beauty of the coast, marking the stage's cultural and scenic conclusion.

 Marismas de Isla Cristina
A tranquil wetland haven for birdwatchers and nature enthusiasts.

 Playa de Isla Canela
A family-friendly beach popular with kitesurfers, offering golden sands.

 Playa de La Antilla
A lively seaside destination featuring vibrant bars and restaurants.

 Paraje Natural Marismas del Río Piedras
A protected natural area teeming with wildlife, showcasing the ecological richness of Andalusia's coastline.

STAGE STORY

The days after completing Stage 76 were a blur of blissful pain. My body ached, but my spirit soared. I was in Lisbon with my good friend Yeni for a few days of post-race relaxation when, over beers and laughter, I jokingly suggested we should run a stage next year. To both our surprise, we woke up the next morning and found ourselves registered for Stages 89 and 90.

Race day arrived, and with it, a nervous flutter in my stomach. This year, I was determined to beat my previous time. My parents, my friend Nicolas, and the ever-enthusiastic Follow The Coast crew were there to support me.

The first rays of sunrise painted the sky in gold and rose as I ran along a deserted beach. The air was crisp and salty, and the rhythmic crash of the waves filled my ears. The course wound through bustling cityscapes, industrial zones, and endless loops that had me retracing my steps. Finally, I was back on the sandy shore, my legs felt powerful, my breath steady. I was in the zone.

After 60 kilometres, I took a quick pit stop—fresh shoes, a couple of espresso shots, and I was ready to continue. My dad joined me for the next challenging beach run. At kilometre 64, we neared a long peninsula. There was confusion about where it began, and whether the crew could reach us with supplies before we were out of range for the next 26 km. An hour later, with energy fading and my water bottle empty, we realised we were stranded. Let the suffering begin!

Just as despair began to creep in, Nicolas, my friend and physiotherapist emerged from the mist. He had somehow run all the way out to us, bringing precious supplies. Not all heroes wear capes—some wear running shoes! My dad, wisely decided to walk back to avoid injury. I couldn't have made it that far without him.

Nicolas and I pressed on, but our renewed energy was short-lived. An hour later, we were once again running on empty. Just when we needed it most, Max and his dog Julien appeared, bearing food and drinks. The four of us made our way to the van, where a much-needed leg massage awaited. The entire crew cheered me on, along with my parents and Yeni's family. I felt a surge of adrenaline, ready to conquer the final 10 km.

As the finish line neared, I realised I was a bit short of the 100 km mark. A quick detour fixed that. The final stretch was a solitary one, as I needed a moment to process the overwhelming emotions—relief, pride, exhaustion, and an indescribable joy. Crossing the finish line, was pure magic. And yes, the tears flowed freely.

Stage 90

LEPE > MAZAGÓN

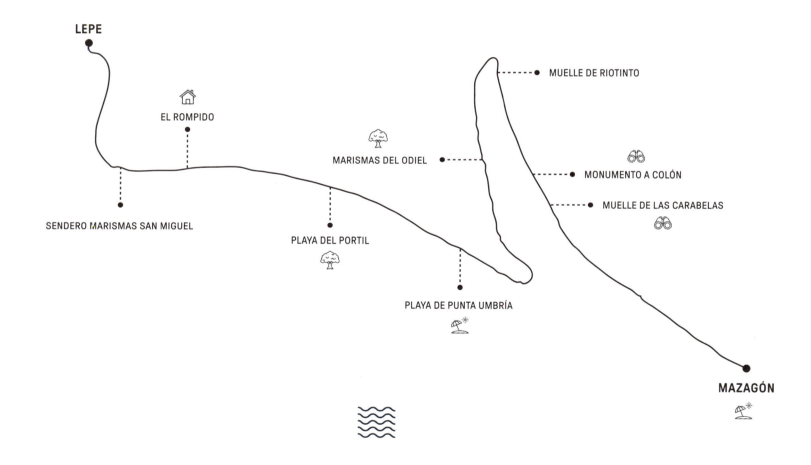

DATE	16/03/2024
DISTANCE	100.1 KM
ELEVATION	302 M
TOTAL TIME	14H51
MOVING TIME	13H21

SHOREHOLDER
Yeni Van den Bergh

ESPIGÓN DE PUNTA UMBRÍA

STAGE HIGHLIGHTS

 El Rompido
A quaint fishing village with twin lighthouses and ferries to Flecha del Rompido, a pristine sandbank surrounded by calm waters.

 Nuevo Portil Beach
Golden sands meet fragrant pine forests, offering a peaceful escape.

 Marismas del Odiel
A UNESCO Biosphere Reserve with unique wetlands and diverse birdlife, including flamingos and herons.

 Playa de Punta Umbría
A lively summer hotspot buzzing with energy, charm, and vibrant seaside life.

 La Rábida Monastery & Muelle de las Carabelas
The site where Christopher Columbus prepared for his historic voyage, where you can find replicas of Columbus's ships.

 Mazagón's beaches
Unspoiled shores and breathtaking sunsets.

STAGE STORY

How I ended up joining Follow the Coast starts with my good friend Simon. He had signed up to run his first stage near Lisbon, and I flew out shortly after to offer some 'post-race care.' Simon had spent six months preparing, even going alcohol-free, so when he crossed the finish line, he was more than ready to celebrate. One evening, after a few cocktails, I jokingly asked him why he'd run 100 km. His answers were inspiring, but when I asked if he'd do it again, he hesitated. In a moment of tipsy overconfidence, I blurted out, "If you do it again, I'll join."

I excused myself to the bathroom, and when I came back, there it was—a screen prompting me to enter my card details. We looked at each other, laughed, and said, "Well, I guess we're doing this..."

Fast forward 10 months, and there we were in Faro, ready for the challenge. Simon had run his stage the day before, finishing with a heroic but emotional effort. The next morning, it was my turn. My mum nervously hovered as I prepared, but there was a hiccup—Max, who was supposed to see me off, overslept. After 20 minutes, he arrived, and I set off, nervous but determined.

The stage wasn't the most scenic. It was mostly 35 km of public beach, 15 km of harbour, and 20 km of bike path along a highway. Mentally, it was gruelling, with no postcard views to distract me—just the rhythm of my feet hitting the ground, hoping for a sighting of the crew van. Every time I saw them, I got a quick laugh, a hug from my mum, and a debate about Milan-Sanremo (we're Flemish, and bike racing is sacred!).

At the 75 km mark, I stopped for my first coffee. I was greeted with a standing ovation from the people at the café. It was a small moment, but it gave me a huge boost.

What made the experience memorable was realising I could handle more than I ever thought possible. With each kilometre, my mind and body found a rhythm, and by the end, I felt a sense of accomplishment I didn't expect. The tough year I'd had seemed to melt away with every step.

Stage 91

MAZAGÓN > ISLA MINIMA

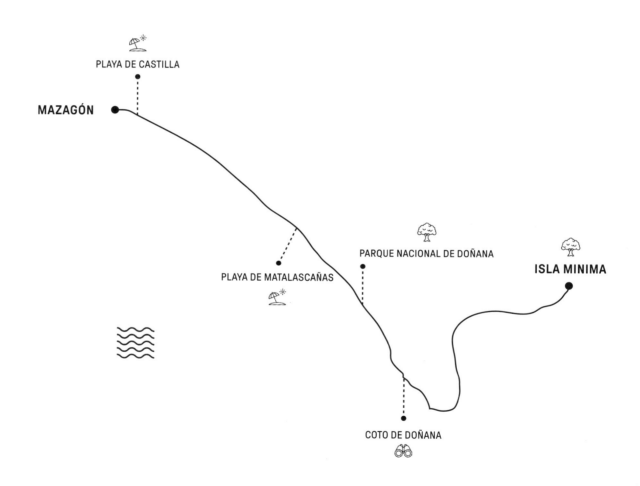

DATE	18/03/2024
DISTANCE	106.3 KM
ELEVATION	286 M
TOTAL TIME	16H15
MOVING TIME	13H40

SHOREHOLDERS
Joost Krijnen
Shiva Zanoli

TORRE DE LA HIGUERA, MATALASCAÑAS

STAGE HIGHLIGHTS

El Rocío
A unique village with sandy streets, Wild West charm, deep equestrian traditions, and an annual pilgrimage, one of Spain's most colourful festivals.

Isla Mínima
A site blending traditional bull-breeding heritage with the beauty of picturesque wetlands and Andalusia's cultural legacy.

Doñana National Park
A UNESCO World Heritage site featuring diverse ecosystems of marshes, forests, and dunes, home to rare species like the Iberian lynx and abundant birdlife.

Playa de Castilla
A pristine stretch of beach framed by dramatic cliffs, offering tranquility.

Playa de Matalascañas
A family-friendly coast destination known for its wide sands and calm waters.

Coto de Doñana
Remote, untouched shores along the coast.

STAGE STORY

Stage 91 was a challenge from the very beginning. We had planned to follow the coastline as much as possible, entering the 'Parque Nacional de Doñana' at kilometre 35 and following the 'Rio Guadalquivir' inland at kilometre 65, aiming for a 117 km finish. We were excited about walking through such an uninhabited stretch, just the two of us. However, the organisation faced major headaches. The national park could only be accessed with park rangers in a 4x4 jeep, and despite Max's months of attempts to contact the conservation organisation, no response came.

The night before, we met to create a Plan B. It was clear that entering the park was impossible. Plan B was to walk the first 20 km along the coast while Max and Gert-Jan headed to the park's visitor centre to plead for permission. At kilometre 33, we left the coast behind, walking 14 km of asphalt road under the scorching sun. We passed the park's entrance, but by then, we knew we couldn't get in. The only option was to continue on the dead-straight road until kilometre 54, where we reached the town of El Rocío, a welcome sight. It felt like stepping into a Western movie, with wooden houses, sandy streets, and horses everywhere. Max and Gert-Jan greeted us with ice cream—a much-needed treat!

Max then directed us to walk a section cutting through the national park, unsure of what would happen. The sandy path became loose, and with every step, we sank ankle-deep. The temperature felt like 37°C, and we were attacked by millions of mosquitoes. The next 15 km felt endless. At kilometre 66, we encountered a tiny black puppy in the tall grass. After some debate, we decided to leave him at the ranch for safety.

Finally, at kilometre 70, we met Max and Gert-Jan again, relieved to escape the mosquitoes. The next stretch was slow; Joost struggled with a foot injury, but with Max's food and encouragement, he pressed on. At kilometre 90, Joost started to feel better, and by kilometre 107, we reached the finish in the dark, tired but happy. Stage 91 had been an unforgettable adventure.

Stage 92

ISLA MINIMA > LEBRIJA

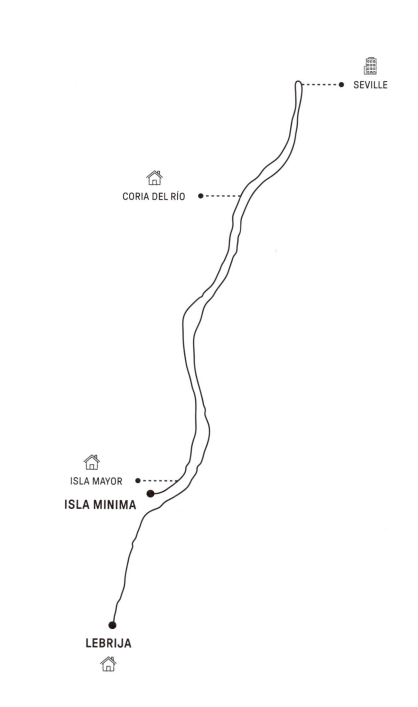

DATE	19/03/2024
DISTANCE	100 KM
ELEVATION	141 M
TOTAL TIME	9H21
MOVING TIME	7H58

SHOREHOLDER
Charles Van Haverbeke

ESTEROS DEL GUADALQUIVIR

STAGE HIGHLIGHTS

 Isla Mayor
A picturesque town surrounded by vast rice fields, a sanctuary for diverse birdlife like herons and storks, perfect for nature enthusiasts.

 Coria del Río
A historic town with a unique connection to Japan, reflecting the legacy of 17th-century emissary Hasekura Tsunenaga, blending Andalusia with Asia.

 Seville
Andalusia's capital, home to the magnificent Cathedral and the Moorish Alcázar, both UNESCO World Heritage sites and architectural marvels.

 Lebrija
A historic town celebrated for its flamenco roots, ancient architecture, and authentic Andalusian charm, offering a rich cultural experience.

STAGE STORY

What moves me most about Follow the Coast is seeing people run their first ultra and create lifelong memories. It's incredible how powerful the 100 km milestone is—it gives people a purpose to fight for, a unique way to bond with loved ones, and a deep journey through body and mind.
Therefore, I find myself slightly torn by my own drive to run a Stage 'on the clock'. For the uneventful Stage 92, I wanted to break the 8-hour moving time or pacing the 100 km at 4:46/km. It's a far cry from the relaxed and non-competitive spirit we cherish and have cultivated. But then I tell myself, "Come as you are"—and part of me thrives on pushing limits.

On the day, being a notorious non-morning person, I arrive late at the start (9 am), but despite the delay, a morning espresso is non-negotiable. The town, seemingly deserted, comes alive in the local Spanish bar, where the brown liquid fuels the spirits of my comrades, local cops included.

The course is an uninspiring U-turn along the Guadalquivir, flowing from the Atlantic to Seville. Yet, instead of a scenic river path, the road is asphalt road cutting vast fields where grain silos emerge from the mist. Mostly, it's a game of dodging trucks and safety rails. It will take a monk's mind to endure the monotony. I plan to start in silence, then settle into the 'waiting room' with podcasts, reserving my animal energy for the final push, fuelled by pounding music. I plan to bank a slight time cushion, running 4:40/km, knowing that at these speeds, seconds matter. Our pit stops are more function than romance—Max handing me food with the efficiency of an F1 crew.

At kilometre 55, the tension between my aching body and the left brain topics of my podcast becomes unbearable. Thankfully, the east bank offers a 40 km stretch of dirt road, where Max and Gert-Jan can support me more closely. Managing heat, absorbing sugar, and easing stomach irritation becomes the real challenge. Max drives ahead, a moving finish line I chase—giving me space, but never leaving me alone.
I landed a 5-minute buffer, but pain starts creeping in. Kilometres 65–80 is my battlefield. Here, belief starts replacing doubt and I enter the euphoric phase. My glassy stare turns is joined by a confident smile—we can do this. Personal pride mixes with deep gratitude for Max's unwavering, intuitive support.

Then, the decompression sets in—the final, hidden challenge. My mind, often anticipating, sees the battle as 99% done, but the last part does matter as much. Eventually, 07:58:00 is the final verdict. We made it.

Stage 93

LEBRIJA > PUERTO REAL

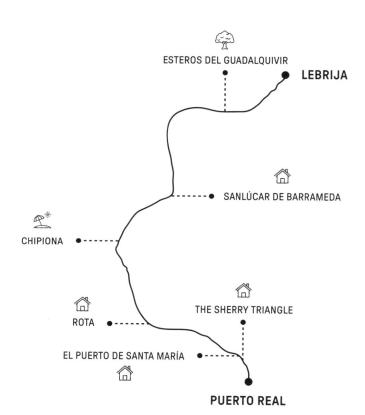

SHOREHOLDER
Adrien Hardy

ESTEROS DEL GUADALQUIVIR

STAGE HIGHLIGHTS

 Esteros del Guadalquivir
Tranquil wetlands teeming with flora and fauna, showcasing the serene beauty of the region.

 Sanlúcar de Barrameda
A vibrant town known for its manzanilla wine, exhilarating beach horse races, and world-renowned seafood served along the riverfront.

 Chipiona
Home to the iconic Chipiona Lighthouse, one of Europe's tallest, and inviting beaches ideal for a peaceful seaside retreat.

 Rota
A historic town featuring the medieval Castillo de Luna, golden beaches, and charming Andalusian streets.

 El Puerto de Santa María
The heart of sherry production, offering traditional bodegas, incredible seafood, and landmarks like the historic Castle of San Marcos.

 Sherry Triangle
A region encompassing Sanlúcar, El Puerto, and Jerez, celebrated for its iconic fortified wines and rich cultural traditions.

STAGE STORY

A few months ago, I decided to take on a monumental challenge: running 100 km. It wasn't just a physical feat; it was an internal journey symbolising resilience and self-transcendence. The goal was clear: to push my limits, test my perseverance, and see how far I could go. But beyond the performance, I wanted to show that, no matter the challenge, the most important thing is to believe in yourself and never give up.

The big day arrived. Excitement, fear, and uncertainty mixed together. As the first rays of sunlight broke through, I set off. The first 50 km went relatively smoothly. I savoured each moment, from flamingos taking flight to sheep grazing on my left.

But from the 55th km onward, muscle fatigue began to set in. Each step became a struggle, and negative thoughts crept in. However, the goal remained clear in my mind. By the 70th km, the endorphins kicked in, and the scenery became even more beautiful with the setting sun.

Then came the wall at the 90th km. Every muscle screamed for me to quit, but the finish line was getting closer. Finally, at 11 pm, after 16 hours of effort, I saw the finish line flag. It was a magical moment when all the sacrifices made sense.

This challenge taught me the importance of perseverance, the power of support from others, and the discovery of inner strength. Practicing mindfulness, learning to appreciate each moment, was one of the greatest lessons. I share my experience in the documentary "Until the Last Kilometre: My Ultimate Challenge," available on YouTube.

A huge thank you to everyone who supported me, especially Max, Constance, Dana, Gert-Jan, Charles, and the entire Follow the Coast team.

I'll end with this quote from Paulo Coelho: "We must do what we've always wanted to do, now."

Stage 94

PUERTO REAL > CAMARINAL

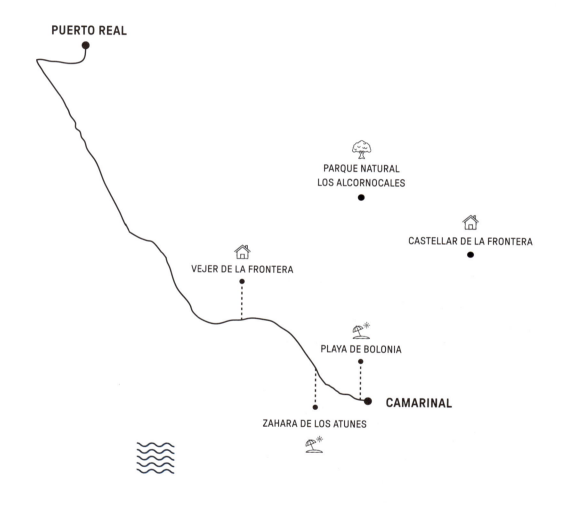

SHOREHOLDER
Ramses De Weerdt

PUENTE DE LA CONSTITUCIÓN DE 1812, CADIZ

STAGE HIGHLIGHTS

 Cádiz
One of Europe's oldest cities, featuring a vibrant old town with narrow streets, lively plazas, the golden-domed cathedral, and picturesque beaches.

 Castellar de la Frontera
A stunning fortified village offering panoramic views of the open country.

 Vejer de la Frontera
A Moorish-inspired hilltop town with whitewashed houses and winding alleys.

 Zahara de los Atunes
Culinary haven renowned for its fresh tuna dish, blending with coast beauty.

 Playa de Bolonia
An unspoiled beach where golden sands meet the fascinating Roman ruins of Baelo Claudia.

 Los Alcornocales Natural Park
A lush natural escape with cork oak forests, offering tranquility and outdoor adventure.

STAGE STORY

After years of dreaming about becoming an ultrarunner and joining the Follow The Coast finishers' wall of fame, the day finally arrived. It was a sunny morning in early spring 2023, somewhere in the south of Spain. I had prepared for the challenge by indulging in some undercooked, bacteria-infested Spanish food—carbon loading for the win! Thirty minutes late to the start, I kissed my fiancée and two strangers in a van goodbye, and set off on my 100 km adventure. I wasn't going to stop until I saw Morocco.

The first marathon went smoothly, at a low pace, passing by flamingos—feeling like one myself. But by the 50 km mark, everything changed. The infamous Spanish salmonella dish came back with a vengeance, and it felt like a double endoscopy without anesthesia. Of course, I had forgotten toilet paper, and from then on, the local fauna and flora flourished. It was a struggle, but recalling my past gastrointestinal experiences in Africa, I remembered the ITG doctor's advice: "Tuc cookies and Fanta will save your life."

At a local beach bar, a refreshing Fanta helped me power through. From 50 to 70 km, I felt like I was flying. Suddenly, a sandstorm rolled in, but I pushed through. I passed a lighthouse, though I was too deep in the zone to appreciate its history. After a quick pitstop for new clothes and a massage, I was ready to conquer a huge mountain during the storm.

But at 80-85 km, I broke—mentally and physically. The sun set, and the cold crept in. I felt like quitting, but a magic combo of caffeine and diclofenac kept me going. It felt like 5 am, but just before midnight, I crossed the finish line—broken but happy.

Three weeks later, my doctor diagnosed a stress-induced heel bone fracture. So, people, please—don't take drugs and run. Exercise is healthy!

Stage 95

CAMARINAL > GIBRALTAR

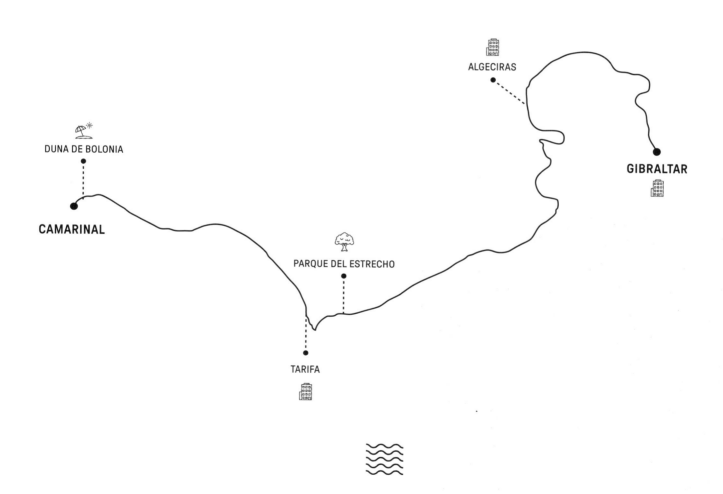

DATE	22/03/2024
DISTANCE	102.08 KM
ELEVATION	2,357 M
TOTAL TIME	10H06
MOVING TIME	9H33

SHOREHOLDER
Michiel Van Der Bauwhede

STAGE HIGHLIGHTS

 Tarifa
A vibrant coastal town known as a surfer's paradise and most Southern point of Spain, with its lively atmosphere, many restaurants and narrow streets, an iconic meeting point of the Mediterranean and Atlantic.

 Algeciras
A bustling port city rich in cultural diversity, serving as a gateway to North Africa and offering a lively urban vibe.

 Gibraltar
A historic site dominated by the iconic Rock, featuring fascinating military history, stunning vistas, and unique British-Spanish cultural influences.

 Duna de Bolonia
A massive natural sand dune offering stunning views and a unique coastal landscape, perfect for nature lovers and adventurers.

 Parque del Estrecho
A protected area showcasing the diverse ecosystems of the Strait of Gibraltar, with breathtaking views and abundant wildlife.

STAGE STORY

The day started off a bit off track. As I followed the GPS to the start, I found the road blocked just 500 m from where I was supposed to meet Max and Gert-Jan. After an hour-long detour, I finally made it, but the start was delayed.

During the ride, I had plenty of time to mentally prepare because the wind that had picked up the day before hadn't calmed down. In fact, it had gotten worse. Birds were stuck in place, trash bags blew across the road, and the palm trees along the coast were nearly touching the ground. It was perfect if the wind was at your back, but after five hours of it blowing in your face, it felt like a different story.

It was shaping up to be the perfect conditions for an epic adventure. Strong winds and sand whipping around, biting at your skin, grinding between your teeth, and irritating your eyes. I felt like Paul Atreides on Dune, venturing into the desert for the first time.

Halfway through, we reached the windmills of Tarifa, the southernmost point of Europe, and at last, the wind shifted. The sand gave way to beautiful natural parks and elevation gains. I could truly enjoy my second stage, having fun from kilometre 55 to 103. After over 90 km, I finally crossed into Gibraltar, even joining a line behind a group of schoolgirls who gave me odd looks due to my exhausted and not-so-fresh appearance (and smell).

Then came the strangest moment of the day: crossing the Gibraltar airport. On both sides, a straight stretch of asphalt stretched out, as far as the eye could see. And that's when I made a mistake! I decided to skip 400 m of the planned route, which led me straight up the famous Gibraltar Rock. Not the best decision after 100 km. My legs ached, and I felt sorry for myself.

But then, I saw the beacon of hope—the Europa Point lighthouse, where Julien and Max were waiting for me. It was an incredible adventure, round 2.0.

Next year, 3.0, 4.0, and 5.0.

↳ Great achievements require great partners. A project like this isn't possible without strong partners that share our vision. Our deepest thanks to ON Running for believing in what we do and supporting us—both logistically and financially. Their commitment allows us to equip our runners with premium Swiss-made gear and to bring this book to life.

More than just a sponsor, ON is a kindred spirit. Together, we celebrate the beauty of design, the power of endurance, and the stories that emerge from the pursuit of both.

A special thank you to the ON Benelux team for their dedication and support.

WWW.ON.COM